FINANCIAL FREEDOM Rx

The Physician's Guide to Achieving Financial Independence

FINANCIAL FREEDOM Rx

The Physician's Guide to Achieving Financial Independence

Chirag P. Shah, MD, MPH
Assistant Professor
Tufts University School of Medicine
Lecturer
Harvard Medical School
Boston, Massachusetts

Jayanth Sridhar, MD
Associate Professor of Clinical Ophthalmology
Bascom Palmer Eye Institute
Miami, Florida

SLACK
INCORPORATED

Senior Vice President: Stephanie Arasim Portnoy
Vice President, Editorial: Jennifer Kilpatrick
Vice President, Marketing: Mary Sasso
Acquisitions Editor: Tony Schiavo
Director of Editorial Operations: Jennifer Cahill
Vice President/Creative Director: Thomas Cavallaro
Cover Artist: Justin Dalton

SLACK Incorporated
6900 Grove Road
Thorofare, NJ 08086 USA
856-848-1000   Fax: 856-848-6091
www.slackbooks.com
© 2021 by SLACK Incorporated

Dr. Chirag P. Shah, Dr. Jayanth Sridhar, *and* Mel Lindauer *have no financial or proprietary interest in the materials presented herein.*

All rights reserved. No part of this book may be reproduced, stored in a retrieval system or transmitted in any form or by any means, electronic, mechanical, photocopying, recording or otherwise, without written permission from the publisher, except for brief quotations embodied in critical articles and reviews.

The procedures and practices described in this publication should be implemented in a manner consistent with the professional standards set for the circumstances that apply in each specific situation. Every effort has been made to confirm the accuracy of the information presented and to correctly relate generally accepted practices. The authors, editors, and publisher cannot accept responsibility for errors or exclusions or for the outcome of the material presented herein. There is no expressed or implied warranty of this book or information imparted by it. Care has been taken to ensure that drug selection and dosages are in accordance with currently accepted/ recommended practice. Off-label uses of drugs may be discussed. Due to continuing research, changes in government policy and regulations, and various effects of drug reactions and interactions, it is recommended that the reader carefully review all materials and literature provided for each drug, especially those that are new or not frequently used. Some drugs or devices in this publication have clearance for use in a restricted research setting by the Food and Drug and Administration or FDA. Each professional should determine the FDA status of any drug or device prior to use in their practice.

Any review or mention of specific companies or products is not intended as an endorsement by the author or publisher.

SLACK Incorporated uses a review process to evaluate submitted material. Prior to publication, educators or clinicians provide important feedback on the content that we publish. We welcome feedback on this work.

Library of Congress Cataloging-in-Publication Data

Names: Shah, Chirag P., author. | Sridhar, Jayanth, author.
Title: Financial freedom Rx : the physician's guide to achieving financial
   independence / Chirag P. Shah, MD MPH, Jayanth Sridhar, MD.
Description: First Edition. | Thorofare : SLACK Incorporated, 2021. |
   Includes bibliographical references and index.
Identifiers: LCCN 2021011965 (print) | LCCN 2021011966 (ebook) | ISBN
   9781630919566 (paperback) | ISBN 9781630919573 (epub) | ISBN
   9781630919580 (pdf)
Subjects: LCSH: Physicians--Finance, Personal. |
   Medicine--Practice--Finance. | BISAC: BUSINESS & ECONOMICS / Personal
   Finance / Money Management | MEDICAL / Education & Training
Classification: LCC R728.5 .S53 2021 (print) | LCC R728.5 (ebook) | DDC
   610.68/1--dc23
LC record available at https://lccn.loc.gov/2021011965
LC ebook record available at https://lccn.loc.gov/2021011966

For permission to reprint material in another publication, contact SLACK Incorporated. Authorization to photocopy items for internal, personal, or academic use is granted by SLACK Incorporated provided that the appropriate fee is paid directly to Copyright Clearance Center. Prior to photocopying items, please contact the Copyright Clearance Center at 222 Rosewood Drive, Danvers, MA 01923 USA; phone: 978-750-8400; website: www.copyright.com; email: info@copyright.com

Printed in the United States of America.

Last digit is print number: 10   9   8   7   6   5   4   3   2   1

DEDICATION

For Meena and Pradip,
for teaching me the value of enough,
and for Steffi,
for reminding me when I forget.

—*Chirag*

For Amma, Appa, Divya, Priya, Arun, and
Mighty Mouse.
What we accomplished, we did together.

—*Jay*

CONTENTS

ACKNOWLEDGMENTS

We are grateful to the following friends and colleagues for critically reviewing this book to help make it better: Mel Lindauer, CFS, WMS; Andrew Lam, MD; Michael Tibbetts, MD; Michael Morley, MD; Charlie Beresford, MBA; Darin Goldman, MD; Sunir Garg, MD; Joe Anaya, MD, MBA; and Ryan Callahan. Thank you to those who offered vignettes for inclusion in the book as well.

We also thank Justin Ma, BS, for expertly preparing the figures.

About the Authors

Chirag P. Shah, MD, MPH is an assistant professor at Tufts University School of Medicine, a lecturer at Harvard Medical School, and vitreoretinal surgeon in Boston. He teaches Financial Literacy 101 at Harvard Medical School, and also to residents and fellows around the United States. He is coeditor of the *Wills Eye Manual, Fifth Edition*, the all-time best-selling book in ophthalmology. He was deputy editor of the American Academy of Ophthalmology's Online News and Education Network, a site that 110,000 ophthalmologists and other health care providers access every month. His professional awards include the Secretariat Award from the American Academy of Ophthalmology and the Senior Honor Award from the American Society of Retina Specialists, awards for outstanding service to the educational missions of both societies. He also won the coveted Ron Michels Award, given annually to the most accomplished graduating retinal surgery fellows in the nation. Dr. Shah was one of 25 medical students nationwide to win the Leadership Award from the American Medical Association. He is the editor of the Clinical Trials section of *Retina Times*, a bimonthly publication read by nearly every retinal specialist in the United States and in 63 other countries. He is well known as a key opinion leader in his field and is an engaging speaker at national and international conferences. He has authored more than 70 scientific papers. An avid marathoner, Dr. Shah enjoys coaching his kids' soccer teams and cycling with his family.

Jayanth Sridhar, MD is the creator and host of the most popular and most listened-to podcast in the field of ophthalmology, *Straight from the Cutter's Mouth: A Retina*

Podcast. He has appeared as a correspondent on CNN, and he also serves as section editor for the American Academy of Ophthalmology's Online News and Education Network. He is a highly sought-after speaker at medical meetings throughout the United States and has earned several honors, including the Secretariat Award from the American Academy of Ophthalmology, the Senior Honor Award from the American Society of Retina Specialists, and the "Best Cool Idea" educational award from the Innovations in Medical Education conference for his podcast. He is a retina surgeon and an associate professor at the top-ranked Bascom Palmer Eye Institute in Miami, Florida, and has authored more than 125 scientific papers. In his spare time, he enjoys traveling with his wife and is an avid basketball fan.

FOREWORD

When there are multiple solutions to a problem,
choose the simplest one.
—John C. Bogle
The Little Book of Common Sense Investing:
The Only Way to Guarantee Your Fair Share of Stock Market Returns

These words of wisdom from my friend and mentor the late John C. Bogle, legendary founder of the $5 trillion Vanguard Group, are at the very core of The Bogleheads' philosophy. Who are the Bogleheads, you ask? The Bogleheads of the internet are a worldwide group of investors who believe in, follow, and promote the low-cost investing advice espoused by John C. (Jack) Bogle. The Bogleheads provide free and unbiased investment help and investor education online at bogleheads.org.

The Bogleheads' principles start with the single most important piece of investment advice you'll need to follow if you hope to attain financial freedom: ***You must learn to live below your means.*** If you don't learn to do that, you'll never increase your wealth and become financially independent, regardless of how much you earn.

Once you've learned to live below your means, here are the other Boglehead principles that are meant to guide you on your path to financial freedom:

- Develop a workable plan.
- Invest early and often.
- Never bear too much or too little risk.
- Diversify.
- Never try to time the market.
- Use index funds when possible.

- Keep costs low.
- Minimize taxes.
- Invest with simplicity.
- Stay the course.

In this book, written by two Boglehead physicians, these guiding investment principles are fleshed out and clearly explained, with particular emphasis on how they relate to physicians and their often unique situations. Investing isn't rocket science, but the investing industry would like you to think it is. By making investing and financial matters appear as too complex for the ordinary investor to understand, financial advisors make their living by offering to handle these complexities by managing your investments for you. However, this investment management comes at a cost—more often than not, by their recommendations of higher-cost products that provide them with a nice living and you with investments that will likely have a hard time overcoming the weight of these higher expenses. Result: The odds are overwhelmingly high that these high-cost investments (and you) will underperform the very segment of the market they're invested in.

While not all financial advisors are to be avoided, some are better than others. For example, a fee-only advisor can provide you with solid advice for an hourly fee; because they don't sell anything except their time, fee-only advisors can recommend appropriate low-cost products and services in an unbiased manner. If you need ongoing investment management, you want to make sure that your advisor's vision is aligned with yours and that the advisor functions as a fiduciary with your best interests at heart.

However, in order for a physician to be able to know what is and isn't good advice, they need to be an informed consumer, and that's where the information proffered in this book comes in. It will take you from ground zero and provide you with the knowledge needed to become an educated investor. Since doctors often have unique needs, this book provides the necessary investment information from a physician's perspective. It explains complex issues in an easy-to-understand manner so that you'll feel comfortable making your investment decisions, whether as a do-it-yourself investor or when selecting and speaking with a financial advisor.

When it comes to sales pitches made by some financial advisors looking for your business, you're apt to hear lines such as "I can get you in on this deal if you act quickly," "This investment can't miss," "You wouldn't operate on yourself, so why would you want to be a do-it-yourself investor?" and, from a friend or coworker, "My guy says he's got a deal that's too good to pass up." These should all be red flags and a sign that it's time to move on in your search for the right investment manager fit.

A good financial advisor will not start by recommending any investment product or service until having conducted an in-depth discussion about your current situation, your risk tolerance level, your wants and needs, your hopes and aspirations, and your plans for retirement and beyond. After all is said and done, simple, low-cost index funds should be the cornerstone, or all, of any portfolio. Since they *are* the market, or segment of the market, they won't underperform. If that's what an advisor recommends for you, you can rest assured that you've found the right one.

Time and money are two precious commodities. Doctors often have too little of one (time) and more than enough of the other (money), and that makes them prime targets for get-rich schemes, so keep your antennas up when the "sharks" come calling. The information contained in this book constitutes great shark protection. So dive right in!

—*Mel Lindauer, CFS, WMS*

Founder and president (2010–2019) of
The John C. Bogle Center for Financial Literacy and
coauthor of *The Bogleheads' Guide to Investing* and
The Bogleheads' Guide to Retirement Planning

John C. Bogle's Words of Wisdom

*Don't look for the needle in the haystack.
Just buy the haystack!*
—The Little Book of Common Sense Investing:
The Only Way to Guarantee Your Fair Share of Stock Market Returns

*The mutual fund industry has been built, in a sense,
on witchcraft.*
—Common Sense on Mutual Funds:
New Imperatives for the Intelligent Investor

*The grim irony of investing, then, is that we investors
as a group not only don't get what we pay for,
we get precisely what we don't pay for.
So if we pay for nothing, we get everything.*
—The Little Book of Common Sense Investing:
The Only Way to Guarantee Your Fair Share of Stock Market Returns

*On balance, the financial system
subtracts value from society.*

—*Enough.: True Measures of Money, Business, and Life*

*The most important of these rules is the first one:
the eternal law of reversion to the mean (RTM)
in the financial markets.*

—*The Clash of the Cultures: Investment vs. Speculation*

*The greatest enemy of a good plan is the dream of
a perfect plan. Stick to the good plan.*

—*The Little Book of Common Sense Investing:
The Only Way to Guarantee Your Fair Share of Stock Market Returns*

*The two greatest enemies of the
equity fund investor are expenses and emotions.*

—The Little Book of Common Sense Investing:
The Only Way to Guarantee Your Fair Share of Stock Market Returns

*Owning the stock market over the long term
is a winner's game, but attempting to beat the market is a
loser's game.*

—The Little Book of Common Sense Investing:
The Only Way to Guarantee Your Fair Share of Stock Market Returns,
10th Anniversary Edition

*The idea that a bell rings to signal when investors should
get into or out of the market is simply not credible.
After nearly 50 years in this business, I do not know of
anybody who has done it successfully and consistently.
I don't even know anybody who knows anybody who has
done it successfully and consistently.*

—Common Sense on Mutual Funds:
New Imperatives for the Intelligent Investor

It's amazing how difficult it is for a man to understand something if he's paid a small fortune not to understand it.

—The Little Book of Common Sense Investing:
The Only Way to Guarantee Your Fair Share of Stock Market Returns

Buying funds based purely on their past performance is one of the stupidest things an investor can do.

—The Little Book of Common Sense Investing:
The Only Way to Guarantee Your Fair Share of Stock Market Returns

INTRODUCTION

Why is it that physicians make $300,000 a year—the top 1% of earners—and yet the majority have a net worth of less than $1,000,000? In fact, 39% have a net worth less than $500,000.[1] Is it because doctors are brilliant scientists and clinicians but terrible with money? Is it because physicians receive little to no formal financial education during their training? Or is it because they typically enter their working years with significant debt? Or, maybe, it's that society expects doctors to live a fancy "doctor's life," and all the pent-up delayed gratification in medical school results in explosive spending immediately after residency?

We believe all of these considerations are relevant. Indeed, physicians graduate from residency/fellowship training nearly $200,000 in debt.[2] Almost half, or 46%, of those aged 35 to 49 years are still paying off student loans.[1] Couple this debt—both the actual financial debt and the financial opportunity cost associated with the training required to become a doctor—with society's perception of the "rich doctor," all within the milieu of the average doctor's inexperience with money, and you have your answer.

I admit, I was jaded toward the end of my neurosurgery residency. I was 34 years old, trying to support a family on $60,000 a year while working 80+ hours a week. My college roommate went to business school and was already a millionaire, while my net worth was –$200,000! And I had been the better student while he partied through college! Soon after I got my first attending job, because of the concept of delayed gratification (and borderline rage), I made my first financial blunder: I leased my dream attending car, a BMW M3. It was awesome. And for those first weeks, I actually felt like a big shot neurosurgeon. But the car cost me over $900 per month, not to mention the ongoing costs of premium gas and expensive upkeep. After a year, I realized that my lifestyle had accelerated so quickly, not just with the car but with a beautiful apartment, two luxurious vacations, a wardrobe upgrade, and a second child, that I was back to living paycheck-to-paycheck, just like when I was a "poor" resident. I should have lived more modestly right out of training and educated myself on where to put my hard-earned salary. I quickly learned from my mistakes. My wife and I created a budget, despite my making what I had initially thought was a lot of money (it is so easy to spend!), and tackled my student loans over the next 5 years while slowly growing our nest egg.

Many doctors, both junior and seasoned, are in desperate need of help with financial management. This book will help physicians at any stage of their careers, from medical students to residents to attendings. It is never too early, or too late, to educate yourself about financial management. For students, residents, or junior attendings, the earlier you start to educate yourself and follow at least some of the principles in this book, the better positioned you will be as you progress through your career. For seasoned attendings, we all have made, or continue to make, financial mistakes, and now is the time to fix them.

The heyday of medicine, when the economic environment was fertile for doctors, is long behind us. Until the mid-2000s, there were relatively low cost-of-living, competition, malpractice exposure, and education and practice costs, along with high reimbursement rates, professional autonomy, income, and high return on investments. After the mid-2000s, there was a profound shift for US physicians away from the aforementioned favorable economic conditions. Compound this with a COVID-19 headwind. Medicine will always be an amazingly gratifying profession, but doctors starting their careers in the current era must master each of the concepts in this book in order to achieve the financial security and freedom of past generations. There is less excess, and thus less wiggle room.

Financial Freedom Rx is a step-by-step guidebook directed toward physicians and their unique financial situation. Most physicians assume debt during medical school, make about a median US salary during training, and then enjoy a several-fold increase in salary later in life as an attending. This book provides specific guidance on where you should put your next dollar depending on where you are along this pathway (see Appendix A). Our goal is to help you achieve financial independence and peace of mind.

The underlying, driving principle of this book is the concept of enough. Enough is what we need to live a happy life. We need enough love. Enough health. Enough time. Enough money. Enough experiences. Enough satisfaction. What is enough for you? Ponder that. The definition of enough is different for different people, and that is something you need to determine for yourself.

Keep in mind that some things, such as time and money, may be inversely correlated for a working physician, as we often earn more when we work more. Unfortunately, there may also be an inverse correlation between your health and your income; we often skip exercise, sleep less, and eat poorly when we are working hard. One must find a balance. This balance is individualized, and may be dynamic, changing as you progress through your career or as your life circumstances change.

When it comes to material possessions, some people need—or want—nicer stuff: cars, houses, furniture, watches, vacations, and so on. Others are content with just enough to make them happy, knowing that the excess money they save will render happiness as they watch their wealth and net worth grow. The concept of "hedonic adaptation" suggests that we each have a happiness setpoint. Despite changes in our environment, we are able to adapt and adjust to maintain a set level of happiness, much like a thermostat maintains a constant room temperature despite changes in the weather. Will more stuff, more money, make us happier? One study found that lottery winners maintained their level of happiness after their financial boon,[3] while another study did find a lasting effect on one's mental well-being after winning a medium-sized lottery prize.[4] So perhaps happiness might not necessarily increase with one's salary, but financial security might impact one's mental well-being.

Attaining financial security as a physician or other high earner does require a conscious effort to not spend it all, particularly if that spending does not directly increase one's happiness. And, to the contrary, excessive spending works against attainment of financial security. Despite the fact that we are hardwired to measure ourselves relative to others in our social group, it is critically important to remember that having enough should be an absolute amount, not relative to what your neighbors have or to how much you think you deserve. Enough is what you need to live a happy life, not an amount that is more than that of the next person. When you eat enough, you are satiated and healthy. When you eat too much, you are left bloated and obese. If you make enough, it doesn't matter that your coresident—or your partner, or your best friend, or your plumber—is making more, you have enough.

Further, enough is how much wealth you need to be independent from a paycheck. It is an empowering feeling to know that your nest egg is large enough to support you and your family for the rest of your days. That financial freedom allows you to live the rest of your life on your own terms: You can work part-time, do more humanitarian missions, teach more, retire, donate future earnings to charity, and so on. Remember, having strong personal connections with friends and family is the strongest predictor of overall happiness and better health. Wealth obviously does not buy friends, but can it buy you time to cultivate close relationships? Would it allow you to work less and play more?

To have enough to be financially independent, one cannot live paycheck-to-paycheck and expect to magically accumulate great wealth. One must live below one's means and soundly allocate the remainder to resolve debt and accumulate savings if one wishes to achieve the peace of mind that comes with financial freedom. In fact, one should consider paying oneself first by tucking away money for savings, then spend the rest, not the other way round. The time it takes to achieve financial independence is based entirely on one's saving's rate, which is inversely proportional to one's spending rate. Of course, as one's salary increases, with stable spending one's saving's rate escalates. Likewise, as one's spending decreases, with a stable salary one's saving's rate escalates.

This book is intended for the average physician, one who places value on tangible things and experiences as well as wealth accumulation and the peace it affords. It is just as helpful for the physician who makes $80,000 per year as it is for the fortunate doctor making $1,000,000 per year. It is not for the uberwealthy, such as the business owner or internet tycoon worth tens of millions who can spend indiscriminately and truly never has to worry about money. Do not compare yourself to this small group of people; you will never keep up! Nor do you need to. There will always be someone with more than you and always someone with less than you. With some financial education and discipline, you will be able to live a purposeful life helping patients while growing a comfortable net worth.

In this book, we take physicians from their first post-training job contract through retirement and cover issues such as resolving debt, saving and budgeting, investment strategies, insurance, estate planning, and common financial pitfalls. Each chapter can be read in isolation, depending on your needs or your stage of life. The totality of the book outlines a comprehensive financial plan for life, giving you the tools you need to understand and apply sound financial principles to steadily grow your net worth. In addition, we have periodically inserted anecdotes from physicians and stories of their individual financial journeys.

There are many other excellent books about personal finance that are worth reading. A few of these include *The Elements of Investing, The Bogleheads' Guide to Investing, The Millionaire Next Door, The Intelligent Investor, The*

White Coat Investor, and *Financial Boot Camp* (see Appendix B). You should continue to read at least one financial book each year to foster your ongoing financial education, just as you participate in continuing medical education in your field.

You will encounter a number of popular investing products on your financial journey. To avoid overwhelming you with an alphabet soup, we want to define some of the more common investing vehicles to help you become more comfortable with the terminology. Don't worry, we realize that these terms and acronyms can be confusing at first. These financial instruments will be described in depth later in the book. They include:

- **Traditional individual retirement account (IRA):** A traditional IRA is an investment vehicle in which one invests tax-deductible dollars that grow tax-deferred. This account is taxed at the time of withdrawal.

- **Roth IRA:** A Roth IRA allows you to invest post-tax dollars that grow tax-free. This account is not taxed at the time of withdrawal.

- **Backdoor Roth IRA conversion:** For those whose income exceeds the limits permitted to contribute directly to a Roth IRA, they can first contribute to an IRA and then convert it to a Roth IRA through the backdoor. This is a way to put more money into tax-free vehicles to grow for retirement.

- **401k:** This is a company-sponsored workplace retirement savings account in which you contribute pre-tax dollars that grow tax-deferred. There is often a company match, meaning your employer will match all or part of your contribution.

- **403b:** Analogous to a 401k, a 403b is the workplace retirement savings account for nonprofit institutions, such as hospitals and schools. Likewise, your investment is tax-deductible and grows tax-deferred.

- **529 educational plan:** These plans allow you to invest post-tax dollars into an educational account that grows tax-deferred. Money withdrawn from this account is tax-free if it is used by the beneficiary for educational purposes. It's a great way to save for college.

- **Health savings account (HSA):** For those who have a high deductible health care plan, an HSA is an account in which you invest pre-tax dollars, they grow tax-deferred, and if you withdraw funds for medical expenses they are tax-free.

- **Real estate investment trust (REIT):** A REIT pools money from a group of investors to invest in various real estate sectors, like commercial or residential real estate.

Before we dive in, a disclaimer: Please remember that we are not personal financial advisors, accountants, or estate-planning attorneys. We are physicians, and are not providing tax or legal advice. For advice specific to your personal financial situation, you should seek professional counsel.

PEARLS

- Physicians are in the top 1% of earners in the United States, yet the majority have a net worth less than $1,000,000.

- Physicians in every stage of their careers can benefit from financial education, just as we participate in continuing medical education in our fields. Consider reading at least one financial book a year.

- Live below your means.

- Pay yourself first, allowing you to spend the rest without guilt.

- "Enough" is absolute, not relative.

REFERENCES

1. Kane L. Medscape physician wealth and debt report 2018. Medscape. May 9, 2018. Accessed April 13, 2021. https://www.medscape.com/slideshow/2018-physician-wealth-debt-report-6009863?src=wnl_physrep_180512_mscpmrk_debt2018&uac=282985FN&impID=1630783&faf=1#1

2. Student debt: ensuring medical school remains affordable. Association of American Medical Colleges. Accessed April 26, 20201. https://students-residents.aamc.org/advocacy/student-debt-ensuring-medical-school-remains-affordable

3. Brickman P, Coates D, Janoff-Bulman R. Lottery winners and accident victims: is happiness relative? *Journal of Personality and Social Psychology.* 1978;36(8):917-927.

4. Gardner J, Oswald AJ. Money and mental wellbeing: a longitudinal study of medium-sized lottery wins. *J Health Econ.* 2007;26(1):49-60. https://www.sciencedirect.com/science/article/abs/pii/S0167629606000853?via%3Dihub

1

Why Financial Planning Matters

Annual income twenty pounds, annual expenditure nineteen and six, result happiness.
Annual income twenty pounds, annual expenditure twenty pounds ought and six, result misery.
—Charles Dickens, *David Copperfield*

Physicians have always worked hard throughout college, medical school, residency, and in practice. Yet we must strive not only to work harder but also to work smarter. We aim to work more efficiently in our practices in an effort to see more patients, take more time off from work, or simply be home in time for dinner. And while we work hard—and smart—our money should work even harder and even smarter.

We rarely have time to learn about financial planning during our medical training; learning it demands a combination of self-study, trial and error, and mentorship. While this book does not replace experience and mentorship, hopefully it will provide guidance for every stage

Shah CP, Sridhar J. *Financial Freedom Rx:*
The Physician's Guide to Achieving Financial Independence (pp 1-7).
© 2021 SLACK Incorporated.

of your career. It is important to have some fiscal literacy as you embark on your career, and continue to become more literate as your wealth grows. As high earners, physicians have the "luxury" of being able to absorb expensive mistakes or outsource financial planning to professionals. However, if you were able to master organic chemistry, you are certainly capable of managing your portfolio. It is important to plan for the future while living a good life. Certainly money does not bring happiness, but it can reduce monetary stress and create opportunities. This defines winning the game: namely, achieving fiscal independence so you can live without financial stress. It does not necessarily mean FIRE—Financial Independence, Retire Early. It means financial freedom and peace of mind. With such peace, would you do more research or teaching, practice in an underserved area domestically or overseas, or work fewer hours so you can go to your kids' soccer games? Would you practice differently, without the conflict of interest inherent within a fee-for-service system? Regardless of your preferences, financial independence allows you to be in control of the rest of your life.

If you are reading this book, you have already taken at least one step (hopefully one of many) toward getting your financial house in order. It is very easy to postpone the many tasks you must complete en route to financial peace, such as considering and purchasing disability, life, and umbrella insurance; maximizing workplace retirement accounts; and utilizing a tax advantaged 529 account for college savings. Step 1 is to actually begin financial planning. Educate yourself by reading financial planning books and blogs and discussing with colleagues and financial advisors. Read this book and use the checklist in Appendix A to ensure you have completed everything that is important to your own personal situation.

In our profession, physicians take care of patients and in the process make a living. In general, the more work you do the more money you make. However, it is erroneous to consider physician income a renewable resource. For one thing, we are all racing against time. As we age, it is common for our productivity to decrease while our practice overhead inexorably and inevitably increases. Further, based on current trends in medicine, reimbursement rates are dropping. In many fields, private equity firms are acquiring medical practices, resulting in significant salary reductions for young doctors and loss of future control of one's practice. With these looming uncertainties of our future earning potential, it is even more important to have a disciplined savings and investment plan from the beginning of our careers. Do not spend tomorrow's dollar today.

Despite the potential forces working against physician income, most physicians still bring in well above the median household income of $56,516 (2016 data).[1] Indeed, the median salary for an internist in 2016 was $196,380.[2] Even the average resident physician in 2018 earned $59,300,[3] slightly more than the median US household income. Of course, these figures need to be put in context by remembering physicians' high degree of student debt and the opportunity cost related to those training years when most highly educated doctors could have been working in far more lucrative jobs. The average physician will complete their residency/fellowship training nearly $200,000 in debt.[4] Physicians devote 4 years to medical school and anywhere between 3 to 8 (or more) years to residency and fellowship training. This opportunity cost is the delay in earning an attending physician's salary and represents lost time for investing and growing a substantial portfolio.

Consider living below your means and placing value on wealth accumulation, just as one may place value on possessions or experiences. Great peace comes from not having to worry about money, but that peace is reliant on a certain degree of self-restraint. You must understand and control your budget, which can grow over time, while trying to make money. On a doctor's salary, you can have almost anything you want, but you cannot have everything you want.

There are several key principles that should be imprinted on your brain to keep you on a disciplined path to financial independence and peace of mind. Just as intentional redundancy got you through medical school, these will be repeated throughout the book:

- Live below your means.
- Have a budget.
- Establish a defensive plan with various insurances.
- Pay off debt.
- Maximize workplace and individual retirement account savings.
- Save and invest consistently; live off what remains.
- Maximize tax advantaged savings (529 plans, backdoor Roth individual retirement account, health savings account).
- Enough is absolute, not relative.

Financial planning does not have to be complex. It does, however, require discipline. You must stick to your plan—during bull and bear markets, despite the temptations of speculative investments or shiny, unnecessary new things. Approach financial planning with the same discipline and rigor you applied to the

United States Medical Licensing Examination. As you are establishing your plan, try to live like a resident for 3 to 5 years after completing your training. This discipline will allow you to eliminate debt, maximize time to accrue compound interest, and establish a sound savings plan. There will be plenty of excess to enjoy later. The following chapters will guide you toward the peace afforded by financial independence.

It was strangely refreshing to know that by my mid-40s I had accumulated enough wealth to no longer depend on a paycheck. It did not require any "sacrifices." I lived a charmed life, with a beautiful home, a reliable Mercedes, and a nice family vacation at least four times a year. How was this even possible when many of my partners were bickering about not making enough and always appeared stressed about money? They owned mansions, costing two or three times more than my house. They bought or leased fancy new cars every 3 years, while I always drove mine for at least twice as long. They owned expensive watches, while my Apple Watch was the most I ever spent on a watch. They flew business class overseas, while I found comfort in coach with a plush neck pillow. They bought their lunch at nearby cafés, while I brown-bagged mine (primarily to eat healthier—but also so I could actually eat on busy days). The difference was tantamount to Nordstrom versus Nordstrom Rack. I did not "slum it" to achieve financial freedom, I just lived more consciously, with much lower personal expenses and significantly greater savings. And in doing so, when many of my partners moaned about decreasing reimbursement rates or increased practice overhead, I didn't care. I shifted my career toward a healthier work-life balance, with more teaching and humanitarian work, while ending my day earlier to spend more time with my family. For me, financial freedom gave me control over my time.

Think of your career and life as a game in which there is a dynamic balance between offense and defense. Early in your career, you should establish and grow a strong defense, including such things as disability and life insurance. Simultaneously, you will grow your offense as you earn an increasing salary and gain stature in your field. As you progress, this dynamic between offense and defense should shift more toward defense again. Asset protection becomes increasingly important as your assets grow. At some point, once you have achieved your financial goals, your focus will be simply not to lose, or at most to keep up with inflation. You will no longer care about winning more. You have already won!

PEARLS

- Financial independence gives you freedom and peace of mind.
- With wealth, you can convert money into time by outsourcing (eg, hiring housekeepers, landscapers, etc).

- Actually get motivated to do financial planning.
- A disciplined savings and investing plan is critical for financial stability.
- Live below your means.
- Live like a resident for 3 to 5 years after completing your training and pay off your student loans.

References

1. Wang J. Average income in America: what salary in the United States puts you in the top 50%, top 10%, and top 1%? (Updated for 2021). Best Wallet Hacks. Updated January 27, 2021. Accessed March 16, 2021. https://wallethacks.com/average-median-income-in-america/#Average-Median

2. How much does a physician make? *US News.* Accessed March 16, 2021. https://money.usnews.com/careers/best-jobs/physician/salary

3. Levy S. Medscape residents salary & debt report 2018. Medscape. July 18, 2018. Accessed April 13, 2021. https://www.medscape.com/slideshow/2018-residents-salary-debt-report-6010044#2

4. 50-state property tax comparison study for taxes paid in 2019. Lincoln Institute of Land Policy and Minnesota Center for Fiscal Excellence. Accessed April 26, 2021. https://www.lincolninst.edu/publications/other/50-state-property-tax-comparison-study-2019

2

Jobs and Contracts

Choose a job you love and
you will never have to work a day in your life.
—Confucius

In medical school, you will "speed date" many different specialties during your clinical rotations in trying to select your future career path. It can sometimes be a challenge to narrow your choice down to one field. There are many factors to consider beyond your clinical interests, including quality of life, years of residency/fellowship training, job prospects, and salary. Just as when choosing a spouse, choose a medical specialty that you absolutely love, one where both you and the field can grow together throughout your career.

If torn between more than one option, consider your future quality of life in terms of hours, stress, and income level. While one is in medical school it may seem easier to calculate the work hours and stress level of a particular

Shah CP, Sridhar J. *Financial Freedom Rx:*
The Physician's Guide to Achieving Financial Independence (pp 9-26).
© 2021 SLACK Incorporated.

specialty than it is to learn salaries. The specialties within the field of medicine are not created equal. For example, the 2018 Medscape Physician Compensation Report had plastic surgery as the highest-paying specialty (average annual compensation $501,000), with 2.5 times the income of the lowest-paying specialty, public health and preventative medicine (average annual compensation $199,000).[1]

Moreover, your perception of the lifestyle in a certain field can be dramatically skewed by your medical school experience. For example, academic neurosurgery can seem like an impossible task in terms of work-hour demands, but there are spine neurosurgeons in private practice who can enjoy a reasonable lifestyle. When deciding on a field, try to look beyond the ivory walls of your medical school hospital and see what life is like out in the real world of practice in order to fully understand how the "average X doctor" lives.

> I thought for sure I was going to be a pediatrician like my mother and take over her practice. However, in medical school, I realized that I loved dermatology and never looked back. Now, nearly 2 decades later, I see that decision was, inadvertently, a smart financial move. I have a great work–life balance as a dermatologist, just as I would have had as a pediatrician, but with nearly double the income.

Once you have chosen a field and completed your training, you can finally get a job outside of the match system. Remember the adage underlying an efficient path to financial freedom: "one house, one spouse, one job." About

50% of physicians will leave their first job (and their first spouse) requiring more time to accumulate wealth. Thus, when it comes to choosing your first job, try your best to choose wisely but remember that it is not an irrevocable decision. Still, there are many important factors to consider as you try to land your ideal job.

JOB LOCATION

Location is often the most important factor when choosing a job, yet it is often the one over which you may have little control. You may wish to settle close to family, or you may need to be in a particular area due to your spouse's job.

If you do have some flexibility, keep in mind that the ability to accumulate wealth can vary considerably based on geographic location. Location certainly influences physicians' salaries. For instance, average physician salaries are nearly $50,000 higher in the north central region of the country versus the northeast. More importantly, the cost of living of a particular region can significantly impact one's savings rate. For example, a $160,638 annual income in Chicago is comparable to a $200,000 income in Boston; this marks a win-win situation for the Windy City, with its higher salaries and lower cost of living. A physician in San Francisco would need to make $254,521, while one in Manhattan would need a staggering $319,947 to maintain a comparable quality of life (Figure 2-1).[2]

Further, state income tax can significantly influence one's take-home pay. California has the highest state tax, 13.3% on seven-figure incomes. Compare this to the income tax–free states of Florida, New Hampshire, Texas, Washington, Nevada, South Dakota, Wyoming, and

Figure 2-1. The cost of living can vary significantly between locations. A $160,638 salary in Chicago has the same buying power as $200,000 in Boston, $254,521 in San Francisco, and $319,947 in Manhattan.

Alaska.[3] With the 2017 Tax Cut and Jobs Act, deductions for state and local taxes are now strictly limited to $10,000 maximum. This further underscores the fiscal value of living in a state with a lower (or nonexistent) income tax rate.

It is also worth considering variation in property taxes based on the location of one's primary residence. Though the average effective tax rate on a medium-valued homestead was 1.395% in 2019, based on an analysis of the largest cities in each state, there are tremendous variations, from 3.30% in Aurora, Illinois, to 0.31% in Honolulu, Hawaii.[4] Keep in mind, however, that the tax rate might not be reflective of one's ultimate property-tax burden due to differences in property values among locations. In other words, one may pay more in property taxes in areas with expensive houses despite a lower tax rate. Thus, you should couch the property tax rate within the context of the cost of living and property values.

If you have the luxury of choosing where you settle, consider the geographic variations in physician salaries, cost of living, and state income and property taxes.

Newly minted residents and fellows might not consider cost of living when choosing a job, but it should be an important factor in choosing where to practice. I would hazard to guess that many physicians in training who have just graduated are quite happy knowing that they will be making a multiple of their fellows' salaries. However, the realities of a mortgage, insurance expenditures, taxes, cost of living, and so on may not have hit home yet. For example, even as a physician, unless your partner or spouse has a lucrative job, it can be quite difficult to establish and raise a family in some areas in California unless one has outside help. The same hard work in a lower-cost city, as I've experienced firsthand, goes much further. If the cost of living is half as much, the income tax is one-quarter as much (or in some cases zero), income is 25% to 50% higher, and the housing is 50% cheaper, it doesn't require any complicated math to figure out that this gives you and your family more options. While I personally would not rank this in the top three reasons why I moved from the West Coast to the East Coast, it is in my mind a top-five consideration. It has given my children more options for schooling in both the present and the future; private schools and 529 accounts both require significant capital. It gives me more options for the future as I age, such as slowing down or retiring earlier than I would have been able to do in a higher-cost city. It gives me more disposable income to support causes that I believe in, to help extended family members, and to spend on creating memories and life experiences with my family. It allows me to invest more now, and through the amazing power of compounding, this will provide more financial flexibility in the future.

Choosing where to practice is a complex and personal decision. It is perhaps one of the biggest decisions one has to make in life. For some folks, none of the things I have mentioned matter at all if they aren't living in a particular city or region. However, for others who may be more flexible, cost of living and finances are factors worth considering because of their impact on personal and family financial planning. Greater financial flexibility certainly doesn't equal happiness, but it usually provides more options. With options, one can make life choices that are meaningful and yield value.

I'm a fool for love! My wife is from New York City and always wanted to return there after our residencies. And not just the City, but Manhattan, one of the most expensive places in the world. We bought a condo, which should continue to grow in value, but the mortgage, condo fees, and maintenance eat up nearly 75% of our combined net income. And we are both supposed to be "rich" doctors! In hindsight,

I wish we had considered living somewhere less expensive. It is very stressful when we have an unexpected expense, like car repairs, and are already very strapped for cash flow. We have been practicing for 8 years and still have med school debt and very little savings. We will have to work for at least 30 years to pay off the mortgage, not to mention college expenses for our kids. And our "retirement account" will be our condo.

SALARY

There can be significant variation in take-home pay based on which job you choose. In general, academic positions will pay less than their private practice counterparts, but every university position has different incentive systems. To complicate matters, pay structures can sometimes be complex, requiring some due diligence to properly compare positions. Signing bonuses, incentive structures, and benefits can vary a great deal between jobs. As you gather job data, financial and otherwise, it may be worth compiling a spreadsheet so that you can make an informed decision. While job satisfaction is also related to other factors like location, intensity of your day, colleague and staff interactions, and commute time, your final earning potential is an important consideration. Remember, however, that excessive income will not beget happiness if it comes at the expense of your physical or mental health.

Signing Bonus

Signing bonuses or moving expenses might not always be offered, but it does not hurt to ask if such a bonus exists. Often there is a significant period of time between the completion of your training and the start of your new job. It is wonderful to have a signing bonus to help cover expenses during this period and avoid depleting savings or accruing more debt. Once expenses for this period are covered, consider applying most if not all of your bonus toward your student loans.

Incentive Structure

There can be significant variation in pay structures between jobs. Some may pay you a fixed salary for a few years before offering partnership, at which point you start buying into the practice for a set number of years, gradually earning a larger percentage of your collections. In other jobs, you may get a fixed salary that increases with seniority, along with certain perks like increased vacation time.

When considering your lifetime salary, it is often more important to consider your final salary ceiling rather than your initial salary. For example, take Jen and Michael, two graduating internists. Jen takes a job that starts at $150,000 annually in private practice and Michael takes a job at $200,000 annually at a managed care system. Michael seemingly has the better deal, right? Not when you consider what happens to those salaries over time. Jen's salary goes up each year with an increasing bonus in the first 4 years before achieving partnership in year 5 with a take-home pay of $400,000. Michael plateaus with his bonus at $250,000. Jen's earnings

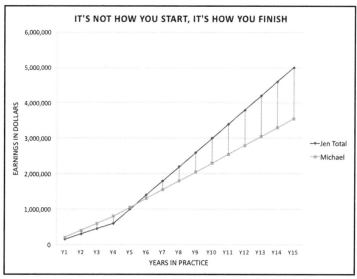

Figure 2-2. Jen starts her career making $150,000 a year, increasing to $400,000 at year 5. Michael starts his career making $200,000 a year, increasing to $250,000 at year 5. Due to Jen's higher ceiling, despite her lower starting salary, she has earned $1,600,000 more than Michael by year 15.

quickly exceed Michael's by year 5 when the lines cross, and by 15 years later she has earned 43% more ($1.6M!). Moreover, this does not even factor in compound interest (earnings on earnings; Figure 2-2).

Benefits

Certain positions will offer superior benefits, such as free or discounted health care for you and your family, child care services, subsidized college tuition for children, and contribution matching for your 401k/403b. Further, there can be variation in the amount of vacation and professional days (eg, for medical conferences) you are allowed each year. All of these perks carry monetary value that should be factored into one's final equation. Additional considerations include ownership options within a group that may include real estate or surgical center investments. Do be mindful, however, of potential conflicts of interest with these investment opportunities and the possibility of increased liability exposure.

My father finished his oncology training at age 32 with four children and one more on the way. He had the options to take lucrative private practice jobs with a large jump in income after 5 years when earning partnership, or an academic position with a similar starting salary but a much lower income ceiling. Because of his love of research and teaching, he took the academic job. By complete accident it ended up being the best financial decision he ever made. When he was diagnosed with cancer 5 years later, he went into chemotherapy with at least the peace of mind that all five of his children would have completely covered college tuition at his university (which we all ended up utilizing). It is impossible to predict the future, but every job carries its own short-term and long-term financial implications and trade-offs.

JOB INTENSITY

You are no longer sprinting from medical school to residency, and from residency to fellowship. Your working career is a marathon, where pace and endurance are critical. As you choose your job, determine what you need to maintain a healthy work–life balance so that you do not hit the wall at mile 20. Sometimes the highest-paying jobs can be the most intense, requiring you to see an overwhelming number of patients at the expense of your health (or sanity). Or perhaps the job is burdensome due to a long commute, a common source of job dissatisfaction. Other elements to consider include the quality of your ancillary staff, intensity of pathology, challenges of the patient population, and esprit de corps of the administrative and medical teams. The culture of a particular practice can significantly influence your happiness, despite how perfect a job might seem on paper.

Like those in many occupations, physicians do not usually choose where they want to practice based solely on finances. Being in close proximity to family or friends, better weather, and returning to one's "roots" are often higher on the list of priorities. That said, being a physician is not a typical job—it can be all-consuming depending on the particular setup of a practice and its surrounding environment. The fact of the matter is that we spend most of our waking hours at work, and clinical practice is work that doesn't always end when the sun goes down. So, if you manage to land in a dream location yet the job leaves something to be desired, it will leave you feeling conflicted, at least to some degree.

PRACTICE STRUCTURE

This will vary by specialty, but there are essentially four different types of practice structures: private practice, traditional academic university employment, managed care system (eg, Kaiser Permanente), and government system (eg, Veterans Administration hospitals). The advantages and disadvantages of each varies between different specialties, but in general there can be large differences in income, practice autonomy, and ownership between these categories of employment.

Private Practice

Private practices often run efficiently, rewarding physicians with higher salaries than the other practice structures. They offer both the opportunity for ownership with a buy-in and greater control over ancillary staff and scheduling. With greater power comes greater responsibility: such positions often require the willingness to grow and develop your practice and to have an active understanding of administration, billing, coding, and other financial details required to run a business. Health care is a highly regulated business with a large administrative component for which you are responsible (and liable) if you are an owner of the practice. Doctors working in private practice might have entrepreneurial opportunities to augment their pay with passive income streams, such as profit sharing from the practice itself, ambulatory surgical centers, and real estate investments.

University-Based Academic Practice

These positions are ideal for academically minded physicians who wish to remain engaged with research and teaching. Both are possible in some private practices as well, but often without the rich resources available to universities. Academic physicians generally have less power to modify day-to-day administration and flow compared to a private practice physician, and salary ceilings are typically lower than those in private practice, although there is great variance between institutions. One potential issue with university-based practices (similar to a managed care system) is the fact that administrative personnel can turn over, and new regimes can bring drastically different policies and philosophies that impact both day-to-day clinical practice and financial incentives. Physicians in university practice may have limited ability to hire or fire the ancillary staff they work with on a daily basis.

Managed Care System

Such systems are often large, multidisciplinary health care systems that strive to provide every health care service to its patient members. Kaiser Permanente is one of the largest and best-known managed care systems, but there are many others throughout the United States. These large managed care systems are growing in certain regions, acquiring more doctors and offices. Such networks can serve as an excellent internal referral network for physicians. However, the physician is essentially an employee and relinquishes the control they would have in a private practice. Some physicians prefer such an environment because they are less engaged with health care management and instead can focus solely on patient care. Physicians in such a system are often salaried, usually making less than their private practice counterparts. However, there may be decent benefits and less intense days compared to private practice. Remember that compensation is negotiable, and it may be worthwhile hiring a lawyer to review and revise a proposed contract and help you negotiate a better salary.

Government System

Working in a system such as the Veterans Administration allows you the gratification of caring for those who fought for our freedom. These jobs tend to be less intense with great benefits and, in general, a very grateful patient population. All of your patients will have health care coverage within the Veterans Administration system. However, some specialized medical or surgical services are not offered within the Veterans Administration system and require preapproval to seek care at an outside center. Similarly to managed care systems, the trade-off here is lower reimbursement and less autonomy over day-to-day activities.

The tenets of this book apply to all doctors and other high earners regardless of the type of practice in which one works. It is certainly easier to realize financial goals with greater income, but a fatter paycheck without a strategic savings and investment plan does not guarantee financial independence. Conversely, a disciplined budget and investment plan, despite a more modest salary, will yield financial security.

PRIVATE EQUITY

Private equity indicates that a business is privately owned and not available for purchase on a public exchange (eg, the New York Stock Exchange). In medicine, the term is often used to refer to a nonphysician investor or group of investors who purchase a practice or hospital. Much as with any other investment, the goal is to maximize returns to investors by increasing current profits and future sale value. Private investors achieve this by lowering operating costs and increasing revenue growth.

Private equity buyouts have increased in recent years in medical fields such as dermatology, radiology, and ophthalmology, and can pose a specific challenge for the early-career physician. Besides changing how a practice functions on a day-to-day basis, a private equity buyout can eliminate opportunities for partnership, which lowers the income ceiling.

Remember the example of Jen, who took a lower starting salary but won the game because she earned a partner level income by year 5? Imagine if Jen's practice were bought by private equity after her third year, and as a result of the changed structure, she was converted into an employee track with a fixed annual salary and bonus of $225,000. Jen's missed opportunity to reach her high-income ceiling would affect a dramatic divergence in her earned income over 15 years (Figure 2-3). Even worse, by taking a lower starting salary with an anticipation of steady increase, Jen would make her income permanently fall behind her buddy Michael.

Our advice for the physician interviewing for jobs is to ask openly if a practice is considering a private equity buyout. Although a verbal assurance may not carry much weight, the response to the question is often telling and may allow for some negotiation in starting salary and in other considerations such as geographic noncompete clauses. For example, some agreements pay non-partner associates a lump sum payment in the event of a private equity sale. It can also be helpful to try to understand the private equity landscape surrounding the practice. Are other practices in the area being acquired by private equity? If referring practices are being bought up by a private equity firm, your anticipated practice might be forced to sell.

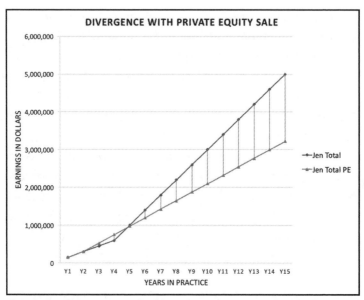

Figure 2-3. If private equity had bought Jen's practice in her third year and capped her salary at $225,000, she would have earned significantly less over her first 15 years of practice compared to what her earnings would have been without private equity.

Noncompete Clauses

A restrictive covenant or noncompete clause, often simply called *noncompetes*, is a clause in your employment contract detailing restrictions on where and how you can practice should you choose to leave your job. There will likely be restrictions on enticing your current patients to follow you to your new job. You will also likely be forbidden to practice within a geographic radius around your current practice for a certain amount of time. Note that this covenant can be restrictive to the point that your signed contract may essentially preclude you from practicing in the same state should you choose to break it.

While noncompetes are technically nonenforceable in some states, like California, the possible legal and political implications (and associated costs) are enough to dissuade most physicians from engaging in a legal battle to stay in the same area. When evaluating a contract, it may be impossible to ask a practice to eliminate a noncompete clause, but there may be some room for negotiation to have a noncompete waived if the practice suddenly changes structure or ownership. One should also remember the impact of a noncompete when evaluating the purchase of a home; making a large financial commitment to a new home and then being forced to sell and move due to a noncompete clause could carry negative financial consequences, especially in a down market.

SEEKING ADVICE

Physicians are experts on medicine, but we are not experts at everything. For many, legal contracts represent the gaps in our knowledge base. Before signing any contract consider consulting trusted mentors, and strongly consider paying to have your contract evaluated by an experienced lawyer for your field of medicine. They can often recognize nuances regarding salary bonuses, benefits, and restrictive covenants shrouded in legal language. Your job is a major investment, so consider the legal fees to review and groom your contract part of that investment.

Pearls

- Location quietly plays a huge role in your ability to grow wealth due to cost of living and state/local tax differences.

- Starting salary is not everything; remember that how much you ultimately make is more important than the initial salary.

- Different practice settings offer pros/cons that must be weighed in the context of your personality and career goals.

- Always have a job contract read by an extra pair of eyes and strongly consider hiring a lawyer to understand all aspects of the agreement.

References

1. Kane L. Medscape physician compensation report 2018. Medscape. April 11, 2018. Accessed April 13, 2021. https://www.medscape.com/slideshow/2018-compensation-overview-6009667

2. NerdWallet's cost of living calculator. Nerdwallet. Accessed March 16, 2021. https://www.nerdwallet.com/cost-of-living-calculator?trk_location=ssrp&trk

3. States with the lowest taxes and the highest taxes. Intuit Turbotax. Accessed March 16, 2021. https://turbotax.intuit.com/tax-tips/fun-facts/states-with-the-highest-and-lowest-taxes/L6HPAVqSF

4. 50-state property tax comparison study for taxes paid in 2017. Lincoln Institute of Land Policy and Minnesota Center for Fiscal Excellence. Accessed March 16, 2021. https://www.lincolninst.edu/sites/default/files/pubfiles/50-state-property-tax-comparison-for-2017-full_1.pdf

3

Initial Steps Post-Training

The first step towards getting somewhere is to decide that you are not going to stay where you are.

—**Chauncey Depew**

GET IT OUT OF YOUR SYSTEM

You made it. Those years of medical school, residency, and possibly fellowship are finally paying off, landing you a great job as a new attending. You will enjoy a major salary hike, probably double or triple your residency salary—and in 2020, a household income of $150,000 puts you in the top 19% of earners in the United States.[1]

It is okay to make a one-time splurge as you are starting out as a new attending, mostly to get it out of your system. Take a nice vacation or buy fancy clothes or do whatever your heart desires, within reason. Then, however, try your best to live like a resident for the next 3 to 5 years as you build your practice and pay off your loans.

Shah CP, Sridhar J. *Financial Freedom Rx:*
The Physician's Guide to Achieving Financial Independence (pp 27-39).
© 2021 SLACK Incorporated.

Your most valuable asset is time. Time, along with discipline and the power of compound interest, will allow you to save a small fortune as you progress through your career. The money you save and invest during those first years as an attending will have the highest expected future value because it will have the most time to compound and mature. Delayed gratification seems to never end; but it will once you grow a comfortable nest egg that lifts the onus of earning an active income from your shoulders.

It's All in Your Head

Becoming financially secure takes a certain mindset. While some people think of saving as a painful form of self-denial, you can also view saving as a powerful form of strength and freedom. Yes, it requires discipline and persistence, but it is also rewarding and satisfying. It feels good to save, and it feels especially good to watch your assets grow and produce wealth (with no work from you) as the cash flows they generate compound. When you realize that being financially secure is a worthy goal that provides a feeling of safety and freedom, it becomes easier to stay disciplined on the path. Passing up the expensive café for a brown-bagged lunch is not hard because you actually prefer seeing your goal of financial independence grow closer. Having power over unnecessary spending is a real form of freedom.

Remember, physicians are conditioned to think *tactically*. "How do I fix this patient's problem?" But we need to think *strategically* if we wish to succeed financially over a 30-year career.

Of course, there are many ways to lose focus. Every day, you are bombarded with hundreds of advertisements and subconscious (and sometimes overt) social pressure to spend or borrow to present a high net worth appearance. But being in control of your financial life is so much better than spending on an object whose allure fades with time.

Take a moment to consider your relationship to money. What does money (or the loss of it) mean to you? How did your family growing up affect your views of money? What fears do you have about money?

Here are some examples of a mindset ready to achieve financial independence:

- You experience satisfaction at seeing your nest egg grow steadily because you know it brings comfort and safety.

- By bringing your lunch to work every day you appreciate that you will save tens of thousands of dollars over the period of your career compared to those who buy lunch every day. And you might eat healthier!

- You enjoy finding a great value—say, an inexpensive ethnic restaurant or a good $10 bottle of wine.

- You enjoy the feeling of walking away from a purchase in favor of saving. You are in control of money, not the other way around.

- You limit impulsive spending. You wait a few days before diving into a purchase and thoughtfully evaluate the pros and cons of that purchase.

- You look at your credit card end-of-the-year summary because you like knowing where your money goes.

- You shop for the best deal on credit card rewards.

- You seek multiple bids whenever you have someone work on or in your home.

- You consider buying a pre-owned car a few years old because you know a new car will lose a significant amount of its value the moment you drive it off the lot.

LIVE BELOW YOUR MEANS

We are all masters of delayed gratification. We work hard during medical school while incurring debt in an effort to again work hard during residency/fellowship training for about the median US salary and then finally enjoy a significant increase in salary, probably double or triple a resident's salary, as a new attending. Be warned: It is easy to fall into a trap; society paints a picture of the "rich doctor" with a big house, fancy clothes, and a luxury car. After delaying gratification during years of grueling education, it is tempting to expand one's lifestyle and expenses immediately upon becoming an attending. However, if you are able to exert some restraint and live like a resident for at least the first several years as an attending, you will be rewarded by the benefits of compound interest and time en route to the peace of mind that accompanies financial independence. Separating need and want is the most important first step in changing your financial future. If you wish to grow wealth, it is helpful to make a lot of money, but it is even more important to live below your means, whatever those means may be, and save a lot. Some authors encourage you to live on half of your salary and save the rest. This number might be aggressive for most, but a reasonable savings rate is anything over 20%, as exemplified in Table 3-1. We will not specify a particular percentage, as everyone's

Table 3-1

YEARS TO FINANCIAL INDEPENDENCE

10% SAVINGS RATE ($30K), $150K ANNUAL SPENDING			
	2%	4%	6%
−$250K	72.5	56.0	48.6
$0	63.3	45.7	36.7
$250K	55.5	38.3	29.8
15% SAVINGS RATE ($45K), $135K ANNUAL SPENDING			
	2%	4%	6%
−$250K	52.2	41.8	36.2
$0	46.3	35.3	29.3
$250K	31.0	30.2	24.3
20% SAVINGS RATE ($60K), $120K ANNUAL SPENDING			
	2%	4%	6%
−$250K	39.4	32.7	28.7
$0	35.0	28.0	23.8
$250K	31.0	24.1	20.0
25% SAVINGS RATE ($75K), $105K ANNUAL SPENDING			
	2%	4%	6%
−$250K	30.3	26.0	23.2
$0	26.8	22.3	19.4
$250K	23.5	19.1	16.3
30% SAVINGS RATE ($90K), $90K ANNUAL SPENDING			
	2%	4%	6%
−$250K	23.4	20.7	18.9
$0	20.5	17.7	15.7
$250K	17.7	15.0	13.1
35% SAVINGS RATE ($105K), $75K ANNUAL SPENDING			
	2%	4%	6%
−$250K	17.9	16.3	15.1
$0	15.4	13.7	12.5
$250K	13.1	11.4	10.2

Note: Stratified by starting net worth and real rate of return, based on a $300K income and 40% effective tax rate.

individual life situation and expense profile are different, but you can determine how your savings rate affects the time it will take to achieve financial independence.

Table 3-1 highlights the number of years until one is financially independent based on one's savings rate, starting net worth, and rate of return. The calculations are based on a $300,000 salary but can be extrapolated for any salary. The savings rate is based on gross income, with an assumption that the effective overall federal and state tax rate is 40%. The table also assumes that you will spend the same amount in retirement as you would while working. This may or may not be true, as you may spend more in retirement because you have time for more activities (eg, traveling, shopping, eating out, health care), or you might spend less (eg, no more mortgage or college payments).

There are two ways to define rate of return: nominal and real. The nominal rate of return is the portfolio return that shows up on your brokerage statement. The real rate of return is that nominal rate of return less inflation. The rates used in this table are real, or inflation-adjusted. The table assumes that you will require 25 times your annual spending to achieve financial independence, with the thought that you will have a 4% draw rate lasting you 30 years. Keep in mind that the earlier you retire, the more years of life you will have left, and so you will have to amass a greater nest egg than is assumed in this table.

Consider Table 3-1 a guide to understanding how your savings and spending rate impacts your net worth. For instance, if you make $300,000, save 20% of your gross income, start your career with a -$250,000 net worth, and earn an average of 4% real rate of return, you will amass 25 times your annual spending and be financially independent in 32.7 years. Now let's see what happens if you increase your savings rate to 30%, meaning you would spend $90K instead of $120K per year. With the same starting negative net worth and 4% real rate of return, it would take you only 20.7 years to be financially independent. Now what if you inflate your lifestyle and save only 10% of your gross income, spending $150K annually with the same negative net worth and a 4% rate of return? You would have to work the rest of your life, as it would take 56 years to retire with the same degree of spending!

Your savings and spending rate is something you can control directly, at least to a large degree, and makes the greatest impact on your net worth and ability to forgo an active income. The more you save, the more you force yourself to live more conservatively. The more you condition yourself to not waste money, the sooner you achieve financial independence. The reason we recommend you save at least 20% of your gross income is that the typical new attending with $250K of education debt making $300K a year could retire after 32.7 years of working, which for most is probably around a typical retirement age in their mid-60s.

To highlight the importance of saving rates, consider the cases of best friends and residency classmates Jane and Kyle. Both of them graduate residency at age 32, take jobs at the same teaching hospital making $150,000 a year, but each adheres to a different savings rate. Jane lives like a resident from day one and aggressively saves 33% of her salary, while Kyle saves only 20%. Assuming a real market return, net of taxes and fees, of 5% for each doctor and interest compounded monthly, Jane will have amassed $2,400,000 after 25 years, compared to $1,500,000 for Kyle—

Table 3-2		
IMPACT OF SAVINGS RATE ON ACCUMULATED WEALTH		
JANE		KYLE
$150,000	Annual Income	$150,000
33%	Savings Rate	20%
$1,673,745.85	Total Savings After 20 Years	$1,004,247.51
$2,424,939.80	Total Savings After 25 Years	$1,454,963.88
$3,388,991.08	Total Savings After 30 Years	$2,033,394.65

a $970,000 difference. Jane's higher savings rate allows her to enjoy more freedom as a physician in her 50s while continuing to utilize the power of compound interest to grow her wealth (Table 3-2).

LIVE ON A BUDGET

Discipline got you to where you are now, and discipline will help you build a comfortable portfolio. Warren Buffett once said, "Do not save what is left after spending, but spend what is left after saving." Budget your savings and your expenses. As your income grows, both your savings and expenses should grow commensurately.

Many of us are accustomed to living on a budget in medical school for fear of incurring more debt with unnecessary discretionary spending. Maybe you consciously brown-bagged your lunch to save money and eat healthy. Or you limited your Starbucks fix to just special occasions. Some of you may have been more sophisticated and kept a more detailed budget on an Excel spreadsheet or a program like Quicken. Embrace your inner nerd and maintain a financial spreadsheet. There are websites online that can help you budget, like Mint or Personal Capital. This becomes even more important as your salary and expenses increase. Remember, of course, there is no need to take budgeting to an unproductive extreme. At the very least, pay attention to irresponsible spending so you are aware of where you can save more if needed.

As a resident, you get a huge relative raise, swinging from paying tens of thousands of dollars in tuition to making about the median US income. That's nearly a six-figure raise! If you have not started a formal budget on a spreadsheet already, now is the time. It can be as detailed or as basic as you wish, but the one number that is absolutely essential to know is how much money you spend each year. What is the cost of living your life? This number will include several big categories such as food, housing, transportation, insurance, retirement, loans (if not deferred), travel, and entertainment. (FYI: If your budget includes docking fees for your yacht, you probably do not need to read this book!) You can be as granular as you would like, but if you use one credit card for your purchases, you might not need to work too hard. Many credit card companies and banks will send you an annual analysis of your spending to help you double-check where your money is going.

Table 3-3 shows a sample budget that a resident might follow. Let's assume her gross income is $60,000 per year, she is single, and lives in Massachusetts, knowing that the tax implications and income will vary based on variables such as marital status, children, and state of residence.

This is a reasonable budget, with a respectable savings rate of 21.9% ($10,000 401k and $3,115 in additional savings, divided by her gross income). As your income climbs through residency and practice, it is important to try to

Table 3-3	
SAMPLE BUDGET FOR A RESIDENT WITH A $60,000 SALARY	
GROSS PAYCHECK	$60,000
401k pre-tax deduction	$10,000
Taxes	$11,285
TAKE HOME SALARY	$38,715
Housing and utilities	$18,000
Loan repayment	$3,600
Food	$6,000
Travel	$3,000
Misc. (clothes, entertainment, etc)	$5,000
Savings	$3,115

live like a trainee for as long as you can. Yes, there will likely be some "lifestyle creep," but if you are able to increase your savings rate as your income grows, the money you saved earlier in your career will have the most time to compound. This is a winning strategy that is likely to allow you to achieve peace of mind sooner rather than later. It is the mindset needed to win the game.

As a resident, I realized the powerful impact that small changes could make on my savings. My wife and I were in Los Angeles, an expensive city that regularly depleted our weekly income. Tired of living paycheck-to-paycheck, I sat down and figured out our current budget. I realized that, between the two of us, we were paying $10 a day for coffee. That was $50 per week and $2,500 per year, which was almost a month of my net income! We decided to each buy a nice thermos ($20), a single-serve coffee machine, and a whole bunch of coffee cartridges. We saved about $4 a cup, or $2,000 per year. And we saved time not having to wait in line for coffee. This exercise was eye-opening for us, a microcosm of what budgeting could do to help us save more money without impacting our quality of life. My wife and I still joke about our coffee budget while we now tackle much larger expenses using the same approach.

A PENNY SAVED IS *TWO* CENTS EARNED

For doctors, most of whom pay close to half their gross salary in taxes, a penny saved is 2 cents earned. If you wish to accumulate wealth, consider creating a budget that includes saving a predetermined dollar amount or proportion of your salary.

With increasing income try to resist the urge to spend more and grow into your income; rather, try to increase your savings with your excess income. Build off your initial budget. With excess income, you will be able to back-calculate how much you need to save per month in an effort to reach your financial goals. Try your best to budget your savings first. Once you have "paid yourself," then use the remaining funds to create an attending budget.

Table 3-4 shows the budget for the same aforementioned person, but now she is an attending. Her salary has ballooned to $200,000 a year, allowing her to maximize her annual 401k contribution and quickly pay down her educational debt. But she continues to live like a resident,

Table 3-4	
SAMPLE BUDGET FOR A NEW ATTENDING WITH A $200,000 SALARY	
GROSS PAYCHECK	$200,000
401k pre-tax deduction	$18,000
Taxes	$56,008
TAKE HOME SALARY	**$125,992**
Housing and utilities	$25,000
Loan repayment	$40,000
Food	$6,000
Travel	$6,000
Misc. (clothes, entertainment, etc)	$8,000
Savings	$40,992

with only modest increases in housing, travel, and living expenses. Her savings rate increases to 29% ($18,000 401k and $40,992 in additional savings, divided by her gross income). However, if she saves an additional $40,000 per year once she has eliminated her educational debt, her savings rate soars to 49%.

PEARLS

- It is okay to splurge a little to buy or do something fun when you start your first job. But then buckle down and live below your means.

- The nominal rate of return is the unadjusted return of your portfolio. The real rate of return is the nominal rate of return adjusted for inflation.

- When you amass 25 times your annual spending, you can draw 4% per year for the next 30 years.

- Your savings rate is something you can control and directly translates into the number of years you need to work to achieve financial independence.

- We recommend that you save at least 20% of your gross income, which would allow you to retire in about 33 years, assuming you have $250K in loans and earn a real return of 4%.

- Budget your savings and expenses. This becomes even more important as your income grows.

REFERENCE

1. Household income percentile calculator for the United States in 2020. DQYDJ. Accessed April 26, 2021. https://dqydj.com/household-income-percentile-calculator/

4

Defense Part 1
Disability, Health, and Malpractice Insurance

Offense wins games . . . defense wins championships.

—Bear Bryant

The path to financial freedom is like playing any sport: you must be willing and able to play both offense and defense if you wish to succeed. Indeed, given their earning potential, physicians are well positioned to win as long as they do not lose. Do not fall into the traps of risky or speculative investments, such as angel investing in start-up companies, unless you have money to spare. If you want to invest in high-risk investments, keep it to a very small percentage of your portfolio. A handsome profit from a risky investment is a nice boon, but always weigh the probability of losing your investment entirely, and how much you will have to work to earn enough to recover. Consider taking the safe path and try not to lose. The boring tortoise who

Shah CP, Sridhar J. *Financial Freedom Rx:*
The Physician's Guide to Achieving Financial Independence (pp 41-50).
© 2021 SLACK Incorporated.

passes unnoticed, without controversy or undue attention, will steadily achieve great wealth and prosperity.

As one's assets and equity grow, remain humble, both out of respect for the majority of the world less privileged than you and for the protection afforded by anonymity. Certainly, become more defensive as you secretly run up the score. This may mean avoiding certain clinical scenarios or procedures that might be more litigious in an effort to decrease your malpractice exposure, or billing conservatively to avoid even the remote possibility of an audit. Or even by scheduling an Uber to take you home from a board meeting so that there is zero chance that the glass of wine you had with dinner will affect your safe return, medically or legally. You may even consider skipping the mogul runs and skiing slower than you did in college so you minimize risk of crashing. Defense, defense, defense.

Insurance is a vital component of your defensive position. As your portfolio grows into a living, breathing, profit-generating beast, you may find that you no longer need certain types of insurance, such as life or disability insurance. You will ultimately become self-insured, investing your insurance premiums rather than maintaining a formal insurance policy. But until then, here we will briefly review the three kinds of insurance you should have early in your career—namely, disability, health, and malpractice insurance.

In Chapter 9, we will discuss life, homeowners, and umbrella insurance. These insurances become more important later in life, when you have dependents, a home, and a growing net worth, respectively.

DISABILITY INSURANCE

Disability insurance is insurance to replace lost income in case you become disabled and unable to work in your chosen profession. For the young physician who has invested sweat, time, and money into earning a high salary, disability insurance is critical to protect against a catastrophic event that not only might cause a tragic physical or mental disability but also financially destroy a doctor and their family. Disability policies can be gotten at any stage in life, but are generally cheaper when obtained at a younger age; we recommend considering a disability insurance policy while in residency training. It is usually much easier and safer to get disability insurance when you are just starting out and are presumably young and healthy. Hospital-specific discounts or reduced rates may also be available for trainees who commit to an insurance policy early.

There are some important points to remember concerning disability insurance. First, here are several riders that you should strongly consider purchasing.

- "Own-occupation" disability insurance is critical for physicians in most specialties. If one is disabled and cannot work in their own occupation, then they are eligible for the monthly benefit even if they find work in another profession or specialty. For instance, if you hurt your back and can no longer operate, you are still eligible for disability coverage while you work a desk job as a consultant.

- Guaranteed insurability or a future purchase increase rider is an important one to purchase when you are young, as it allows you to increase your policy coverage with increased income without repeating the medical clearance exam and under-writing process.

- Residual disability is a rider that allows one to receive partial benefits in the setting of partial disability.

- A cost-of-living rider allows your monthly benefit to increase with the cost of living; this is more impor-tant for younger physicians should they become disabled at a young age and have to collect disability insurance for a number of years.

- Noncancelable, guaranteed renewal means that your insurance company cannot cancel your policy if you pay your premiums. And if your insurance company folds, it is required to sell your policy to another company.

Second, both disability insurance premiums and monthly distributions are dependent on your current level of income (most policies limit the payouts to a percentage of your current earnings, eg, 60%). If you are a high earner, you can consider having more than one disability policy to maximize your benefit in the event of disability. You might want to consider maxing out your policy when you are young, to the limits of your income. As your income grows, you can increase the amount of your monthly dis-ability benefit. This typically requires you to submit proof of your increased income to your insurance company, usually a copy of your recent W-2 form.

If you purchased a guaranteed insurability rider, which we recommend, then you do not need to undergo another medical examination as you did when you first applied for disability insurance. Keep in mind that your annual premium will be less when you purchase coverage at a younger age when you are less likely to become disabled.

However, a disability at a young age before you have had the chance to grow a robust portfolio would be most devastating, hence the need for disability insurance.

One consideration for disability insurance is whether to utilize pre- or post-tax dollars to fund your policy. The advantage of using pre-tax dollars is that this is yet another mechanism to reduce your taxable income; however, if you do end up dependent on your policy's pay-out, your benefit is now fully taxable as income. We recommend to simply use after-tax dollars to ensure that if you become disabled you have the maximum tax-free benefit given disability insurance's role as a fail-safe in case of catastrophe. If your policy pays 60% of your pre-tax income in post-tax dollars, that is effectively the same take-home amount when factoring in taxes (40% tax rate).

Third, certain dangerous hobbies (rock climbing, ultra-light plane flying, etc) can preclude you from obtaining disability insurance. Given the number of years you have invested in becoming an attending physician, it simply makes sense to play it safe and avoid high-risk activities that could preclude you from practicing medicine. Any injury, particularly an avoidable one, would be tragic. A big part of your defensive plan should be playing it safe, especially when in the vulnerable financial period of residency training.

Fourth, when a disability insurance policy is activated, there is typically a waiting period of at least 3 months before you begin collecting the monthly benefit. The disability policy will kick in after that, often with monthly payments to the age of 65 years, depending on the exact policy. That means having an emergency fund is critical since there will be a 3- to 6-month period without income before your disability policy is activated. Hopefully, you have an accurate understanding of your budget, as discussed in Chapter 3. Your emergency fund should be highly liquid and stable; most keep this money in cash in a bank account. We are conservative and recommend enough savings to cover your living expenses for 6 months. This covers you, not just if you become disabled, but also if something happens and you switch jobs and have a period of no income. If all goes well, you will never have to touch your emergency fund, but it serves as the cushion between the period of initial loss of income and the start of disability benefit payments.

Do keep in mind that because the disability benefit typically stops at the age of 65 years, you must allocate a proportion of your disability benefit to save for retirement. Given that the average life expectancy is only increasing, this means you may incur a few decades of expenses beyond the period your disability benefit will last. This further reinforces our thesis that you should try to grow your nest egg early in your career for more protection in the case of future disability.

I developed a traumatic fourth nerve palsy after falling off a bicycle on vacation. It gave me intractable double vision when looking straight ahead. I learned to adopt a head tilt to help mitigate my double vision. This injury made it impossible for me to work as an otolaryngologist. Fortunately, I had a good "own-occupation" disability policy that continues to give me a monthly benefit that allows me to live my life. Of course, I did not ever expect to stop practicing medicine, but at least my injury did not spell financial doom for my family and me.

> I now work as a consultant, while also teaching medical students. My disability benefit, coupled with my earnings, more than replaces my lost salary as a practicing physician.

How long will you need disability insurance? Until you have the financial means to be self-insured. Disability insurance is expensive, especially when you add more coverage after residency to protect your growing income. It would not be uncommon to spend $5,000 to $9,000, or even more, every year for disability insurance, depending on the age at which you enroll, your health, your coverage, and the number of riders you select. Further, some high-earning physicians will layer on an additional policy to come closer to replacing their monthly income. When you are financially independent, you have enough to live the rest of your days completely independent of your work income. This is when you no longer need disability insurance. If you become disabled and are no longer able to work and earn as before, you do not need a monthly disability benefit to live your life. Once you have enough, it would be worth allocating your disability premium toward a nice family vacation or additional savings and dropping your disability policy altogether.

HEALTH INSURANCE

Health insurance for you and your family will almost always come from your or your spouse's employer. It will usually cover catastrophic medical events in the case of a major unanticipated injury or hospitalization. Further, it should also cover medications, wellness checks, and routine medical screening, with physical exams and tests if needed. There may be a deductible or co-pays for care you access. If so, consider utilizing your employer's health care flexible spending account option to designate pre-tax dollars for anticipated medical expenses. In 2020, you could allocate up to $2,750 pre-tax. This money can be used for co-pays, eyeglasses, contact lenses, anticipated dental work, and so on. Keep in mind that you must spend the allocated amount in your flexible spending account or you lose it, so do not overfund. You have until March of the following calendar year to spend it.

Remember that if you are between jobs (eg, between the end of your medical training and the start of your life as a full-fledged attending) you may have gap periods without employer coverage. You are typically offered COBRA (named after the Consolidated Omnibus Budget Reconciliation Act), which allows you to temporarily keep your health coverage after employment ends. COBRA insurance is generally expensive, as you are now paying not only your portion of the premium but also the employer's share. Still, it may be worth it, particularly for those with families. At bare minimum, have catastrophic coverage to keep yourself and your loved ones out of financial danger should one of you have a medical emergency during a gap period.

MALPRACTICE INSURANCE

Similar to health insurance, malpractice insurance will typically already be established when you join a group. If you are going solo or doing contracting/consulting work without coverage, it is critical to have some sort of malpractice coverage. Every state has slightly different rules on malpractice damages and protections, and these laws are in constant evolution. Important considerations include whether the policy is claims made (covers only when the claim is made) versus occurrence (covers only when the claim occurred) and whether you need "tail" coverage to cover claims after your policy has ended or you are no longer practicing.

> Being sued was the worst professional experience of my life. One of my patients was injured due to a medical error in the operating room. It was an emotional and political nightmare. Even though I was not at fault, the experience rocked me to the core and made me question whether it was still worth trying to help patients in an imperfect world that demands perfection. I never before had bothered to check on the details of my malpractice insurance; it turned out I had excellent coverage through my employer. I am indebted to my malpractice carrier, who assigned me an amazing lawyer. We met many times in preparation for my deposition. I know lawyers are expensive, but I wasn't charged a penny for his time. I was eventually dropped from the claim, as he expected all along. I cannot tell you how relieved I was for the case to be over, but I will forever be hardened as a result. Getting sued was a horrible experience, one that would have been even worse without good malpractice coverage.

PEARLS

- When it comes to finances, you must think defensively, even before you develop a strong "offensive" game.

- Get disability insurance as a resident, with the following riders: own occupation, guaranteed insurability, residual disability, and cost-of-living adjustment. Increase your coverage as your salary grows.

- Your employer will likely provide health and malpractice insurance. Have some knowledge of your coverage. Understand that in gap periods of employment you will either have to elect to pay for COBRA insurance or obtain short-term catastrophic coverage.

- Consider utilizing a flexible spending account to tuck away pre-tax dollars for medical expenses.

5

Student Loans and Retiring Debt

What can be added to the happiness of a man who is in health, out of debt, and has a clear conscience?
—Adam Smith

It can be daunting to start your practice with a significant amount of debt, but this is the reality for most doctors. We encourage you to retire student debt with the same discipline that you will soon use to grow your portfolio. Before tackling student debt, be sure never to carry credit card debt beyond your statement due date. These high interest rates will compound quickly and crush you. If you are reading this while carrying credit card debt, please return this book and wire the refund to your credit card company.

Shah CP, Sridhar J. *Financial Freedom Rx:*
The Physician's Guide to Achieving Financial Independence (pp 51-66).
© 2021 SLACK Incorporated.

Credit cards are like crack. I couldn't get enough trying to play the credit card game to score airline miles. I would open several new credit cards just to capture thousands of airline miles, which I then used for free trips and hotels. It was a great deal for a poor medical student. But what I also did was use one credit card to cover the balance of another. The combination of multiple cards and transferred balances was painful. Ultimately, I had to pay a lot in interest, and my credit score nose-dived. (I didn't realize this until I applied for a home loan years later.) I have since learned from my mistakes. I now have one credit card that puts 2% of my expenses directly into my Fidelity account, and I pay the balance automatically every month. It's probably too conservative in comparison to my colleagues who successfully manage the credit card "game," but the miles/points are not nearly as important to me at this stage of my life and career.

Although physicians boast higher incomes than the average American, they start further behind. The average debt for an allopathic medical student graduating in 2018 was $188,758, according to the Association of American Medical Colleges (AAMC).[1] Osteopathic medical students reported a median school loan debt of $265,000 in 2018.[2] Compare that to the personal debt of the average American ($38,000 excluding mortgages as of 2018).[3] More sobering is that 13% of graduating allopathic medical students surveyed by the AAMC in 2018 reported having more than $300,000 in debt.

The rules surrounding federal loans, loan forgiveness programs, and debt repayment options are ever-changing. Please refer to the list of useful links to government websites at the end of this chapter for up-to-date information to help you eliminate student debt.

Federal Versus Private Loans

Student loans are issued either by the federal government (direct loans) or via private companies (private loans). Maximize direct loans first, as they offer lower interest rates and opportunities for federal forgiveness post-training. The 2020–2021 cap on a Federal Direct Unsubsidized Loan for medical students is $47,167 if enrolled in a year-round program. (This amount is prorated for a program less than a full 12 months.) As another option, with a Direct PLUS Loan you can borrow up to the cost of attendance of your particular school, minus any financial aid. Federal loans have benefits of deferment, forbearance, consolidation, death and disability cancellation, and loan forgiveness. Private loans have no hard cap but higher interest rates and do not qualify for forgiveness programs.

Student loans must be used specifically to pay for education and student living expenses. One advantage to student loans is they cannot be foreclosed on, but they do not discharge (disappear) with bankruptcy, and they generally carry higher interest rates than other types of loans, such as home mortgages.

ADDRESSING YOUR STUDENT DEBT

For students starting a Federal Direct Unsubsidized Loan between July 1, 2015 and July 1, 2016 (ie, the medical school class of 2019), the interest rate was 5.84%.[4] Private loans have even higher rates. Given the significant aggregate interest rate on your student loans, getting rid of your debt early in your career gives you a guaranteed return on your money. Paying down your debt will allow you to finally achieve a net worth (total assets minus total debts) of $0 and continue to grow a positive portfolio. Also, there are psychological benefits to being debt-free. Residency, fellowship, and then the first few years of medical practice can be stressful enough without a growing financial albatross hanging around your neck. Definitely meet with the financial aid officer at your medical school before you graduate, or with a student loan advisor, to review your options and formulate a plan to eliminate your student debt.

I was the first member of my family to go to college, and I did it with a full need-based scholarship to our local state school. For medical school, I had to take both federal and private loans and graduated $150,000 in debt. I planned to pay it off as soon as I started residency, but then life got in the way: My husband and I were expecting our first child, and paying off debts seemed close to impossible on a resident's salary. So we let them sit. We had no idea about repayment plans that could have helped make monthly payments more palatable. My loans grew only slowly during my 4 years of residency and with it developed a gnawing sense of dread. Worse still, my husband was still in school at the time with large student loans of his own.

We thought that once I started my attending job, we would really start making a dent in those loans, but between moving expenses, child care expenses (now for three beautiful children), and unexpected medical expenses for our last child, we hardly made a dent. Our marriage began to suffer; the constant mental stress of thinking of our loan burden and the monthly reminders in the mail were causing us to bicker and fight. Those 2 years after residency were the hardest years of my life, and much of it was caused by our significant student debt.

Finally, by my third year of being an attending, we had righted the ship financially and began aggressively paying off our debt. Though we lived like residents for the next 3 years, we were so much happier and at peace together, feeling that we had a brighter future to look forward to. Six years out of my residency training, we are now debt-free and looking to purchase our first house. It has been a long road, but we made it together. If I had one piece of advice for bright-eyed 27-year-old me coming out of medical school, it would be to start paying off that debt right away. I would have read about repayment and forgiveness programs and created a workable action plan.

GOOD VERSUS BAD DEBT

Some kinds of debt are "good," particularly low-interest debt with tax-deductible interest, such as a home mortgage. Your investment portfolio might be able to beat this low interest rate, in which case it is better to pay the minimum toward the debt and invest the rest, assuming you have the discipline to invest the difference. For example, assume you secured a home mortgage with a fixed 15-year rate of 4%, and your index fund portfolio returns an average of 8% that is compounded over the years. In this case, it makes sense, even after accounting for tax deductions on your mortgage interest and capital gains taxes on your index funds, to carry your mortgage debt for the full 15 years and invest any excess savings in a total stock index fund. Keep in mind that this calculation is based on assumptions; simply paying off loans is rarely a "bad" idea. Further, paying off a 4% mortgage is a guaranteed return of 4%, as opposed to a historical stock market return of 8%. Again, psychologically, for many it can ease stress to simply pay off debt.

Unfortunately for medical professionals, the Federal Direct Unsubsidized Loan interest rate and other student loan rates are generally not low, so paying off student loans is usually a high priority relative to investing. For most, the only investment worth considering before or while simultaneously paying off your student loans is a pre-tax contribution to your retirement account up to the level of the match offered by your employer. Such "free money" is hard to pass up, assuming you are in a position to start saving some money for retirement.

Minimizing Debt in Medical School

Start before enrolling by factoring finances into your choice of school. Consider attending the least expensive medical school you can, and go to a school in a more affordable city. Medical school scholarships exist; find them and apply for them.

As a medical student, live modestly. Living below your means is technically impossible as a medical student because, barring family support, an unusual lucrative side hustle, or a financially successful significant other, your means are essentially zero. However, you can often spend less by sharing an apartment with a roommate, buying used books and equipment, owning a bike instead of a car if feasible in your area, packing your own lunch, and discovering cheap or free recreational activities.

Avoid falling into the trap of "keeping up with the Joneses" in medical school. Many of your classmates may be spending freely, but they may have significant family support or just have no concept of the financial pain waiting at the end of the medical school rainbow.

Service Scholarships

There are a few programs that will cover part or all expenses in exchange for years of service post-training. For example, the Health Professions Scholarship Program will cover medical school tuition and expenses for the same number of years that one must serve post-training. A separate military match is required for residency. The Indian Health Service scholarship will cover up to $40,000 in student loans in exchange for 2 years of service post-training in an area serving American Indians or Alaskan Natives and is open to allopathic and osteopathic medical students as well as optometrists, dentists, nurses, and pharmacy students. One can apply as late as the final year of residency.

The National Health Service Corps has two options: a scholarship similar to the Health Professions Scholarship Program that covers years of medical school in exchange for years of service and a loan repayment program that pays up to $50,000 in student loans in exchange for 2 years of commitment. Service is done at a designated National Health Service clinic in a designated area of need. Another option is enrollment in a dual MD/PhD program at a medical school; generally, tuition is free and a stipend may be provided for living expenses.

The catch with all these programs is that you must invest a significant number of years after your training working at a less profitable job than the one you would otherwise take and living in a location that might not be desirable for you and your family. Further, the duration of the service commitment is time that you would otherwise spend toward a partnership track in a private practice or academic medical center. Thus, enrolling in any of these programs without a specific interest in the potential job or location might not be a viable strategy for most. However, if you already have an interest, this is a wise and noble way to reduce or even eliminate your student loan burden.

CONSOLIDATION AND REFINANCING

Consolidation refers to the process in which different federal loans are grouped together as one large loan. The interest rate of this loan is obtained by averaging the interest rates of the individual loans. As such, consolidation does *not* lower the overall interest rate. Keep in mind that consolidation will reset the clock on loan forgiveness (more on this later).

In contrast, refinancing only applies to private loans. The process of refinancing is complex, but essentially the reason one would refinance would be to change the terms of a loan to a lower interest rate that could be paid off over a different period of time. To qualify for refinancing at a lower interest rate one generally must demonstrate good credit.

INCOME-DRIVEN REPAYMENT

In residency you will start repaying your loans. There is a strategy. First, refinance any private loans you have. Second, consolidate all federal loans to obtain a single interest rate. Third, look into income-driven repayment (IDR) programs and federal forgiveness programs. Remember that when you start with your federal loan, you are given the 10-year standard repayment plan with monthly payments. IDR programs allow monthly payments to be modified to a lower level based on your income and family size, making meeting monthly payments more realistic and feasible on a resident's salary. There are several options for IDR programs, the most recent iterations being Pay As You Earn (PAYE) and Revised Pay As You Earn (REPAYE; Table 5-1).

PAYE caps payments at 10% of your discretionary income and allows married physicians to file taxes as Married Filing Separately, which may reduce required payments. Payments are capped at the standard 10-year repayment plan level, which limits how much your payments would increase as an attending. The catch is that it will take *longer* to pay off debt. One is only eligible for PAYE if (a) one borrowed for the first time on or after October 1, 2007, (b) a federal loan was received on or after October 1, 2011, and

Table 5-1

PAYE Versus REPAYE

	PAYE	REPAYE
Requirements	Must have … • Partial financial hardship • Received a federal loan on or after October 1, 2007, and have had no outstanding federal loans at that time • Received a long disbursement on or after October 1, 2007, or consolidated on or after that date	• Anyone with qualifying federal loans is eligible
Payment Amount	• 10% of discretionary income, but never more than on the standard, 10-year plan	• 10% of discretionary income, with no cap; payments could be higher than would be on the standard plan
Consideration of Spouse's Income	• No, if filed separately	• Yes, even if filed separately
Repayment Period	• 20 years	• 20 years if you have only undergraduate loans • 25 years if you have any graduate school loans
Interest Subsidy	• The government pays 100% of unpaid interest on subsidized loans in the first 3 years of repayment	The government pays… • 100% of unpaid interest on subsidized loans in the first 3 years of repayment • 50% of unpaid interest on subsidized loans after the first 3 years, and on unsubsidized loans at any time
Capitalization Limit	• If disqualified from PAYE due to increase in income, or failure to recertify your income annually, the amount of unpaid interest that can be capitalized is limited to 10%	• No limit to the amount that can be capitalized

(c) if the monthly payment amount determined by PAYE is less that what one would pay under the standard repayment plan.

REPAYE is similar in the sense that it caps payments at 10% of discretionary income; however, there is no cap on payments, meaning these payments will generally increase significantly once you hit attending income. While you will pay off debt faster, these payments could be hefty during that time period. REPAYE is unique in that it offers an interest rate subsidy, effectively reducing interest rates for physicians-in-training. This is a gift.

Which is better between PAYE and REPAYE? This is a complex question that depends on your circumstances. First, are you married? Married residents will prefer PAYE, while single trainees will lean toward REPAYE. Second, do you want to pay off debt quickly with more expensive payments (REPAYE) or slowly with more strictly capped payments (PAYE)? While the latter sounds enticing, REPAYE allows you to pay off debt faster, and the interest rate subsidy can be significant, cutting interest rates almost in half. On the other hand, PAYE has the benefit of limiting the amount of unpaid interest that can be capitalized to 10% of your entering loan balance (see Table 5-1). Why is that good? Capitalization of interest means that unpaid interest is added to the balance of a loan, potentially increasing in a compounding fashion the amount of interest owed. Compound interest working against you is a bad thing! So limiting the amount that can be capitalized can be very beneficial in reducing the overall payment amount. To summarize, we would recommend REPAYE for most physicians given the benefit of faster debt repayment and the interest rate subsidy, unless one is married to a high earner and/or is enrolled in a loan forgiveness program and wants to keep loan payments as low as possible. Regardless of which of the two plans you select, there is no prepayment penalty if you choose to pay off your loans sooner than is outlined in the plan.

PUBLIC SERVICE LOAN FORGIVENESS

Loan forgiveness programs allow debt to be "forgiven" after a certain number of years of payments. The most popular forgiveness program is the Public Service Loan Forgiveness (PSLF) for direct loans (federal loans). Forgiveness of federal loans via PSLF can relieve you of tens of thousands of dollars of debt. Loans from private lenders do not qualify for PSLF.

The biggest benefits of PSLF are (a) that the final forgiven loan is not considered as income and is thus tax-free, (b) you are eligible after 10 years of payments (120 payments), and (c) you can count small IDR-level payments during your training toward these 10 years. For example, after completing a 5-year residency during which you paid 60 small IDR-level payments, it would only take you 5 more years to achieve loan balance forgiveness. The only requirement/catch is that all 10 years of payments must be made while you are employed full-time by a non-profit (501[c]3); otherwise, you are not eligible for PSLF. Therefore, it is important to know that all of your training hospitals or institutions qualify. Ensure that you receive your paycheck from a 501(c)3 institution, and not some outside entity; it is important to remember that even if you work at a 501(c)3 institution, your paycheck might not come from the same qualified institution. It is also important that your first attending job qualify as a 501(c)3 institution, such as an academic medical center or Veterans Administration hospital.

PSLF rules are strict and the program has a high rejection rate; as such, it requires careful planning and documentation to take advantage of this resource. You can track your progress toward your 120 qualifying payments on the Employment Certification for Public Service Loan Forgiveness Form (https://myfedloan.org). If you choose to go for PSLF, we recommend having a back-up plan, both psychologically and financially, if your PSLF application is rejected or if Congress changes its policy and PSLF is no longer available.

LOAN DEFERMENT DURING TRAINING

There are programs that allow either deferment or forbearance of federal student loans. Both deferments and forbearance still mean that interest accrues on unsubsidized loans, and forbearance also has the extra penalty of interest accruing on subsidized loans. Deferments are usually granted to trainees in cases of economic hardship, and the period of deferment lasts from 6 months to a maximum of 3 years. Forbearance can be obtained by anyone in residency training.

The major disadvantages of either of these types of programs are accruing more interest and postponing the ability to get PSLF earlier by not making payments during residency/fellowship via an IDR program. It is well worth trying to meet these minimum payments if you think you will be working for a qualifying nonprofit organization post-training for at least a few years to hit the 10-year mark and get your remaining federal loan balance forgiven tax-free.

Aggressively Crush Student Loan Debt Unless You Are Going for Public Service Loan Forgiveness

Live like a resident, budget accordingly, and aggressively attack debt. You have the benefit of a six-figure salary; now use it to go above the minimum payments and get rid of your debt. The goal should be to eliminate debt as soon as possible, and ideally within 5 years.

In our opinion, the only situation in which it does not make sense to aggressively pay off student loans is if you are hoping to achieve federal debt forgiveness with PSLF. In this case, the goal should be to meet minimum 120 payments over 10 years and then apply for forgiveness. Jobs that qualify for PSLF are typically academic or government-based and may well pay less than private practice positions. If one is choosing a lower-paying job at a 501(c)3 institution to be eligible for PSLF and not for more important reasons like job satisfaction, they should do the math for their own personal situation to determine if obtaining loan forgiveness is financially worth the trade-off of a lower income during those early career-building years.

Retiring Debt Versus Investing

There are differing thoughts on this issue, but in general we recommend retiring debt as quickly as possible. Significant debt is not only a psychological burden but high-interest debt can also be a snowballing financial burden. There are, however, some scenarios that favor investing over eliminating debt when one does not have enough cash flow to do both simultaneously. For instance, it is financially prudent to invest in a workplace retirement account up to the company match so that one can capitalize on this "free money." Also, a low-interest mortgage might be debt worth carrying, as the interest is tax-deductible (if greater than the standard deduction) and if one's anticipated investment returns exceed the mortgage interest rate. Realistically, when earning a six-figure salary and budgeting a lifestyle below one's means, it should be possible to concurrently meet the employer's match while paying off student loan debt.

PEARLS

- The average medical professional carries significant amounts of student loan debt far above the debt of the average American.

- Dealing with student loan debt begins with being frugal and thrifty in professional school to minimize the amount of loans required.

- Residency is an excellent opportunity to begin paying off debt via IDR programs that can make monthly payments feasible and carry future benefits. These include PAYE and REPAYE, which carry different pros and cons depending on one's marital status and planned time to full debt repayment.

- Federal forgiveness programs may be an option to explore when one plans to work at a nonprofit organization (such as an academic medical center or governmental hospital) as an attending.

- Attendings should pay off debt aggressively, only prioritizing meeting the company match via a 401k/403b retirement plan before eliminating student loan debt, ideally within 5 years after finishing training.

HELPFUL RESOURCES

- https://studentaid.gov/understand-aid/types/loans/subsidized-unsubsidized
- https://www.medicineandthemilitary.com/joining-and-eligibility/medical-school-scholarships
- https://www.ihs.gov/loanrepayment/
- https://nhsc.hrsa.gov/scholarships/index.html
- https://studentaid.gov/manage-loans/repayment/plans/income-driven
- https://students-residents.aamc.org/financial-aid/article/public-service-loan-forgiveness-pslf/
- https://hms.mediasite.video.harvard.edu/Mediasite/Play/59c0ba2d9d784f68a3fb70f4de048cd21d

REFERENCES

1. Medical student education: debt, costs, and loan repayment fact card. Association of American Medical Colleges. October 2018. Accessed March 16, 2021. https://store.aamc.org/downloadable/download/sample/sample_id/240/
2. Survey of graduating seniors summary: 2017-2018 academic year. American Association of Colleges of Osteopathic Medicine. Accessed April 17, 2021. https://www.aacom.org/docs/default-source/data-and-trends/aacom-2017-2018-academic-year-graduating-seniors-survey-summary-report.pdf?sfvrsn=e14d2197_6
3. Leonhardt M. Here's how much debt Americans have at every age. CNBC Make It. August 20, 2018. Accessed March 16, 2021. https://www.cnbc.com/2018/08/20/how-much-debt-americans-have-at-every-age.html
4. Advocacy & policy. Association of American Medical Colleges. Accessed March 16, 2021. https://www.aamc.org/advocacy-policy

6

Tax-Advantaged Investing

The stock market is filled with individuals who know the price of everything, but the value of nothing.

—Phillip Fisher

The next two chapters are rich with strategies for you to grow your wealth, first by discussing how to max out all tax-advantaged vehicles, and then by describing how to utilize taxable vehicles. Do not be overwhelmed by the alphabet soup of available investment buckets. The anecdotes help ground the concepts and make them easier to absorb. Consider these two chapters as resources you will revisit often as you shape your portfolio.

WHERE TO PUT THAT NEXT DOLLAR

Those with high incomes have the ability to make some financial mistakes and still achieve financial independence

Shah CP, Sridhar J. *Financial Freedom Rx:*
The Physician's Guide to Achieving Financial Independence (pp 67-85).
© 2021 SLACK Incorporated.

in a reasonable time. As a new attending there will be a number of people trying to help you grow your portfolio, offering you potentially high-fee (eg, whole life insurance) or high-risk (eg, angel investing) opportunities. But with a little education, you should have a framework within which you can determine where you should put that next dollar. The following is a brief outline, which we will then discuss in further detail. It is not necessarily a linear outline, as you may contribute to several buckets at once. For instance, you may prioritize paying off your 7% interest rate student debt while simultaneously maximizing your retirement plan contribution to capitalize on your company's match. You will need to do some homework to determine precisely what is most financially sound for your own individual situation. Consider consulting with your accountant or financial advisor, particularly if your financial situation is complex.

- Maximize workplace retirement plan contributions up to the match (free money!).

- Pay off high-interest loans, such as student loans and credit card debt.

- Maximize retirement plan contributions past match/ without match (assuming there are good options).

- Invest in an individual retirement account (IRA) versus backdoor Roth IRA, depending on your income.

- Evaluate 529 accounts for education savings if you have children.

- Consider health savings accounts (HSAs) if available from your employer.

- Plan your taxable investing strategy.

WORKPLACE RETIREMENT PLANS: 401K, 403B, 457

Your workplace retirement plan is often the first investment instrument you will use to grow your personal portfolio. Workplace qualified retirement plans have two huge benefits: contributions to the plan lower your tax bill now, and even more importantly, this non-taxed money grows tax-deferred until you start withdrawing it (probably when you are in a lower tax bracket in retirement). Plus, many plans have a matching contribution from your employer. All of these benefits create a big "tailwind" for growth. It is not uncommon for a retirement plan to grow to more than seven figures during your lifetime if you max out your retirement plan.

It makes a lot of sense to contribute to your workplace retirement plan as soon as possible, hopefully as early as your internship year. Your institution's 401k (for profit) or 403b (nonprofit) workplace retirement plan is one of the best vehicles to help you save, assuming that there are reasonable, low-cost funds within the plan in which you can invest. For those with a governmental employer, and for some with certain nongovernmental employers, a 457 plan functions similarly to a 401k or 403b plan in some ways. Some of you may have the option of having an HSA as well. Your 401k, 403b, or 457 contributions are pre-taxed dollars, so you will not feel the full pinch of this investment in your paycheck. Further, the dividends are not taxed as they are reinvested, allowing greater growth than a taxable account by avoiding "tax-drag." Tax-drag is the reduction in return due to annual taxes that "drag" a taxable portfolio's growth, compared to one that is tax-sheltered. Keep in mind you do pay ordinary income taxes when you withdraw the money in retirement, but possibly at a lower tax bracket if you have less income then.

A big advantage is that your employer may have a match, also known as "free money," to accelerate the savings in your workplace retirement account. The match puts money into your retirement plan up to a certain percentage of your income. Determine how much is matched by your employer to give you a benchmark of how much you should try to contribute. We strongly recommend that the first place you put your money is into a workplace retirement plan at least up to the match. This is an immediate 100% return, as your contribution is doubled. You should even consider making this contribution a higher priority than paying down your student loans, as an immediate 100% return beats the interest you are paying on your loans. As you are able, try to maximize your annual 401k, 403b, or 457 contribution to the annual limit set by the Internal Revenue Service (IRS). It was $19,500 in 2021.

For those with a 457 plan option, it is possible you may also have a 401k or 403b option. In this case, you can contribute up to the maximum annual limit for each plan, thereby doubling your total annual pre-tax contribution.

For those who are age 50 or older during the current tax year, each 401k, 403b, and 457 plan allows for catch-up contributions, in addition to the annual limit for those younger than 50. In 2021, the catch-up limit was $6,500, making the total limit $26,000 for anyone at least 50 years old. For those with both a 401k and a 457 plan, the catch-up contribution applies for each plan, allowing one to contribute a total of $52,000 in 2021 between the two plans.

One difference between 401k/403b and 457 plans is that the former two plans carry a 10% penalty if one withdraws money before the age of 59½. On the other hand, there is no penalty for early withdrawal from a 457 plan. However, nongovernmental 457 plans can be lost to creditors in case of the bankruptcy of your employer, can only be rolled over to another nongovernmental 457 plan if you switch jobs (and your new job has that option!), and have differing distribution rules. For example, some nongovernmental 457 plans require a lump sum distribution, while others allow spreading of the distributions over years. This distinction has critical income tax implications and should be understood prior to investing in your employer's 457 plan.

> My company's 401k plan is a painless way to save for retirement. I contribute the maximum amount every year, which was $19,000 in 2019. My employer automatically deducts my pre-tax contributions over my 12 pay periods each year, so I'm contributing about $1,584 per month. However, because this is pre-tax and I pay about 40% in taxes, my take-home income only goes down $950 a month. I don't even notice this amount missing from my paycheck, mostly because I am so accustomed to paying myself first. After 25 years of this strategy, I have accumulated well over $1,000,000 in my 401k retirement account. I will likely be in a 25% tax bracket in retirement, allowing me to eventually live off 75% of this account.

Some institutions offer a Roth 401k plan, which means you pay taxes now and allow your contribution to grow tax-free until retirement, at which time you can withdraw from this account tax-free (ie, the compounded growth in a Roth plan is not taxed—very nice!). This does allow you to tuck away more money now. This is because the post-tax dollars you contribute to a Roth 401k are not taxed upon withdrawal. If you contribute the same amount of pre-tax dollars to a traditional 401k, you would have less than you would in a Roth 401k because the traditional 401k distributions are taxed. Your post-tax Roth 401k account will effectively be much larger in retirement than a traditional 401k, because you do not owe any taxes on the former. This allows some tax diversification when withdrawing money in retirement. Strongly consider investing in a Roth 401k plan if you can afford it and do not expect to be in lower tax bracket in retirement.

The after-tax Roth 401k contribution may be too much for some to afford now. Furthermore, if you think you will be in a lower tax bracket upon retirement, it may make more sense for you to contribute to a traditional 401k. A Roth 401k is probably a good idea for those with sizeable annual savings whose portfolio returns in retirement will keep them in the highest tax bracket. An important consideration is assessing your current state's income tax. Residents of California who plan to retire in Florida would be much better off with a traditional 401k plan than a Roth 401k plan.

As a resident, retirement planning was not even on my radar. I didn't know the first thing about 401ks. I was so busy working and taking care of our new baby that I didn't take the time to educate myself about retirement accounts. Even if I had, we were probably not in a position to tuck money away for retirement; we needed all of my income to make ends meet. It turns out, my hospital had a great match for 401ks, and I missed out on it. When I got my attending job, I was still ignorant about 401ks, and missed out on a partial match for a couple of years until I finally felt I had enough cash flow to start saving for retirement. I not only left money on the table for 6 years but got a late start in retirement savings and missed out on some tax-advantaged years, but I was able to right the ship. I now maximize my 401k contribution and benefit from a partial match. I'm back on track.

One relevant issue to keep in mind is that many 401k/403b retirement plans allow the employee to select a percentage of their salary to invest into the retirement plan each pay period rather than an absolute amount. This requires one to do the math to ensure that the maximum contribution amount is met each year. For example, a physician with a salary of $190,000 should designate that 10% of their salary be contributed to their 401k to meet the 2019 maximum of $19,000. The tricky part comes if you are fortunate enough to hit an unexpected bonus for the year and this is added to your salary. The first year in my university position, I made $25,000 as bonus that I did not anticipate and actually ended up overcontributing to my 403b as my contribution percentage did not take the extra income into account. I had to pay a small penalty when filing taxes. To avoid this problem going forward, I now keep my contribution percentage lower than necessary for the first half of the year. When the biannual bonus is paid out in July, I readjust my percentage for the second half of the year to ensure I get exactly $19,000 without ever going over again. The lesson is that it is critical to figure out the bonus system in your organization and when this bonus is typically calculated and paid. Keep this in mind, as once money is contributed into the retirement account, it cannot be retroactively removed or changed without penalty.

Some early career attendings are concerned about investing money in an "untouchable" retirement plan versus saving for a property purchase. It is true that withdrawal is generally penalized if contributions (not earnings) are withdrawn prior to age 59 years, 6 months for a working adult, or prior to 55 years old for a retired adult. However, there are certain exceptions that allow for early penalty-free hardship withdrawal of contributions:

- Down payment on first residence purchase
- Higher education fee due in the next 12 months

- Large unreimbursed medical expenses for an individual, spouse, or dependents
- Eviction or foreclosure on one's home

ROTH INDIVIDUAL RETIREMENT ACCOUNT

A Roth IRA is an excellent means of tax-free savings for retirement, allowing you to invest post-tax dollars now for tax-free withdrawal later. The contribution limit for a Roth IRA was $6,000 in 2021 for those younger than 50 years of age, and $7,000 for those 50 years or older. Most attending physicians, however, have a modified adjusted gross income (MAGI) greater than the 2021 maximum income limits. Those who file taxes as single, head of household, or married filing separately if they did not live with their spouse during the year can contribute the full amount if they made less than $125,000. If their income was between $125,000 and $139,999, they can make a prorated contribution to their Roth IRA. If their income exceeded $140,000, they cannot contribute. Those who are married filing jointly, or qualifying widows/widowers can contribute the full amount if their income was less than $198,000. Contributions are prorated for incomes between $198,000 and $207,999, and are not allowed for incomes beyond this limit. For individuals who are married and filing separately, and lived with their spouse at any time during the year, contributions are prorated for incomes between $0 and $10,000 (yes, this is a very low amount), and disallowed for greater incomes.

Because of the income requirements, a Roth IRA is worth considering as a resident, if it fits in your budget, or as a first-year attending, if you do not exceed the maximum income requirement for that calendar year.

For instance, if you are younger than 50, single, and made $30,000 during the first 6 months of 2021 as a senior resident, took a month off, and then made $80,000 during the last 5 months of the year as an attending, your annual income of $110,000 would allow you to contribute $6,000 to a Roth IRA.

Backdoor Roth Individual Retirement Account

Given that most physicians have the fortunate problem of exceeding the Roth IRA income limits, consider a backdoor Roth IRA, which has no income limit. The term "backdoor" makes this strategy sound suspicious, but it is an accepted and completely legal vehicle to save for retirement in a tax-efficient manner. It involves contributing post-tax dollars to a traditional IRA, and then converting it to a Roth IRA. There is no tax on the transferred money as long as you do not have other IRAs (eg, SEP-IRA [simplified employee pension individual retirement account]) and that you do not exceed the annual contribution for a backdoor Roth IRA. A Roth IRA grows tax-free and it is not taxed at the time of withdrawal. Put a reminder in your phone to do this once a year. You can immediately convert the money in a traditional IRA to a Roth IRA.[1]

The maximum annual contribution for a backdoor Roth IRA was $6,000 in 2021 for those under 50, and $7,000 for those 50 and older. You have until Tax Day to make a contribution for the prior year. This means if you have never done a backdoor Roth IRA conversion, and it is between January 1 and Tax Day in mid-April, you can contribute for both the prior and the present year. If you are doing this for yourself and your spouse, and you have the means, you could put away $6,000 for each of you for 2020 and $6,000 for each of you for 2021, for a total of $24,000 in Roth IRAs between the two of you.

Keep in mind that not every physician can cleanly contribute to a Roth IRA if they have money in a tax-deferred IRA in their name. These types of IRAs include SEP-IRAs, traditional IRAs, and SIMPLE IRAs, but do not include 401k or 403b accounts. For those with a tax-deferred IRA, the backdoor Roth IRA conversion triggers taxes per the IRA aggregation rule, and the taxes are determined on a pro rata basis across all accounts. For example, if one has $54,000 of existing pre-tax IRA funds in place and contributes $6,000 of post-tax dollars to a traditional IRA, they cannot convert just the $6,000. Since their $6,000 post-tax contribution is only 10% of the $60,000 total IRA money, the Roth IRA conversion will be treated as $600 of post-tax dollars (10% of $6,000) and $5,400 of pre-tax dollars (90% of $60,000); this $5,400 is taxable at the time of conversion. Due to their existing pre-tax IRA money, a backdoor Roth IRA conversion no longer makes sense due to the tax costs.

There are ways to work around this and still contribute to a Roth IRA if you have an existing pre-tax IRA account. You can roll over your existing IRA into an employer's 401k plan if that is accepted by your plan. Alternatively, if you earn some income as an independent contractor, you can roll your SEP-IRA into an individual 401k. The other option is to pay taxes on the conversion, which might only make sense if you have very little in existing pre-tax IRA accounts, and/or are a resident in a low tax bracket. Finally, you could convert the entire traditional IRA balance into a Roth IRA and pay taxes, which often would be too costly due to taxes depending on the exact amounts.

Likely, the most common existing IRA that complicates participation in a backdoor Roth IRA for physicians is the SEP-IRA. The SEP-IRA is a nice way for a physician who earns some income as an independent contractor or sole proprietor to save for retirement. Physicians who earn money as independent contractors, for instance as consultants, expert witnesses, or moonlighters, receive compensation that is recorded on Form 1099. Approximately 20% (18.6% until you max out your payroll tax) of this sole proprietor income can be contributed to a SEP-IRA using pre-tax dollars up to $58,000 per year (2021 limits). This upper limit is far greater than the $19,500 limit on 401k contributions in 2021 through your workplace retirement account. The SEP-IRA, like your workplace 401k, grows tax deferred until taxed at the time of withdrawal.

> It was important for me to maximize all of my tax-advantaged savings options, given my huge tax burden every year. I earn the greater majority of my income practicing medicine, but I do some consulting on the side to help boost my income. Years ago, I opened a SEP-IRA account to siphon off some of my pre-tax earnings as a consultant, tantamount to how I contribute to a 401k plan through my medical practice. What I didn't realize at the time was that a SEP-IRA would complicate my ability to participate in a backdoor Roth IRA. Some of my colleagues who consult a lot advised me to let the backdoor Roth IRA go, as it was "only" $6,000 in 2019. But I felt this would add up over

time, especially because this amount would be tax-free in retirement. So I had to do a fair amount of work to make the backdoor Roth IRA happen while still preserving a pre-tax retirement account for my consulting income. The first thing I did was open a self-employed 401k, also known as an individual 401k or solo 401k. It was not as simple as opening a SEP-IRA and required a phone call to Fidelity and the completion of some forms. I also had to get an employer identification number online. I then had to roll over my existing SEP-IRA into my new self-employed 401k. I learned that Vanguard does not allow such a rollover but Fidelity does, so I switched brokerages. Once I closed my SEP-IRA, I no longer had any pre-tax IRA accounts and could participate in a backdoor Roth IRA conversion every year. After going through the 1099 forms detailing my consulting income, my accountant tells me how much I can contribute to my self-employed 401k each year. Though it did require some work to open a self-employed 401k and roll my SEP-IRA into it, including switching online brokerage companies, it was worth it to me to fund a backdoor Roth IRA account.

Self-Employed 401k

For physicians who earn at least part of their income as independent contractors/sole proprietors, and also wish to participate in the backdoor Roth IRA conversion, it might be best to roll over an existing SEP-IRA into their employer's 401k plan or into a self-employed 401k. This is also known as an individual or solo 401k. Moving forward, any pre-tax retirement contributions from their sole proprietor income should be contributed to a self-employed 401k, and not a SEP-IRA.

It is relatively easy to set up a self-employed 401k through most brokerages such as Fidelity or Vanguard (though Vanguard does not allow SEP-IRA rollovers into their self-employed 401ks). You will need an employer identification number (EIN), which can be attained online on the IRS website using form SS-4.

Aside from allowing one to participate in a backdoor Roth IRA, a self-employed 401k has several advantages over a SEP-IRA. In 2021, a self-employed 401k allows one to contribute a maximum of $58,000 per year, the same as a SEP-IRA, but they can max out an individual 401k at lower income levels. Within the self-employed 401k you can designate up to $19,500 of your contributions as Roth contributions, meaning you would fund this with post-tax dollars. A post-tax $19,500 that grows in a tax-protected manner is worth more than a pre-tax $19,500 that gets taxed upon withdrawal. The self-employed 401k allows catch-up contributions of $6,500 per year for those over 50, for a total of $64,500, compared to no catch-up contributions for SEP-IRAs.[2] Further, you can take a loan, if needed (we hope not!), from a self-employed 401k and not from a SEP-IRA. Finally, most states afford the same asset protection from creditors for 401ks and SEP-IRAs, but at least two states (Minnesota, South Carolina) give additional protection to 401ks.[3]

529 ACCOUNTS

As you well know, higher education is not cheap and it is not getting any cheaper. Per the College Board, the average annual tuition and expenses (fees, room and board, and allowances for books, supplies, transportation, and personal expenses) for a 4-year private college was $54,880 in 2020–2021. Public 4-year college expenses for in-state students was less but still a hefty $26,820.[4] These numbers are projected to skyrocket, based on the current college inflation rate, to more than $80,000 per year for private colleges and $45,000 per year for public colleges by 2033.[5] 529 accounts allow you to save for your child's or children's higher education expenses in a tax-efficient manner. You contribute post-tax dollars that grow tax-free, and this value is not taxed upon withdrawal if used for educational expenses. You can withdraw up to $10,000 per year for elementary, middle, and high school expenses, and as much as needed to cover college and graduate school expenses.[6] Qualified expenses include tuition, room and board, books, and computer expenses.

You can contribute up to the annual gifting amount per year, which is $15,000 per gift per child in 2021. This means you and your spouse are allowed to gift each child $30,000 in post-tax dollars per year without paying estate taxes or eroding your nontaxable estate limits upon your death. In other words, this gifting amount is in addition to the estate limits you can leave tax-free upon your death. Alternatively, you can make a one-time contribution of 5 years'-worth of gifts, or $150,000 in 2021, as long as you do not give the same individual another gift for 5 years. It should be noted that you can directly pay educational expenses for your children without counting against your annual gift tax exclusion. Consider dollar cost averaging your

529 contribution every week or month as you would for your taxable investments. These 529 accounts are also an excellent way for grandparents or other family and friends to make tax-efficient gifts toward future educational expenses.

How much should you contribute? There are many variables that make forecasting your child's educational future difficult. One can never predict if their child will get a college scholarship, attend a more affordable state school versus an expensive private school, or choose a path that does not involve college. Or will they go to medical school and incur 8 years of tuition? Or will all medical schools be free by then (we hope so!)? All you can do now is make your best guess and try to optimize the tax-saving advantages of a 529 plan without grossly overfunding it. As a crude calculation, the rate of growth of tuition is roughly equal to the expected 7% to 8% growth of your 529 account. So, if you wanted to fully fund college, stop contributing to the 529 when the value equals the 4-year cost of college in that given year. If you choose to withdraw any amount for reasons unrelated to higher education, you will incur a 10% penalty. If you overfund the account, it can be transferred to others, such as grandkids, nieces, or nephews. It cannot be donated to charity.

We started funding 529 accounts for both of our kids soon after they were born. In those early years, we did not have enough extra cash to put much away, but we did the best we could. As our salaries grew, so did our annual 529 contributions. This was one of the smartest things we could have done for their college education. With their 529 accounts we funded almost all of their college expenses by the time they started. And we greatly benefited from the tax-free growth. It was a huge reduction in stress to know that funding college was practically done when each left for school. Our 15-year mortgage also came to an end around the same time. No college expenses and no mortgage! We were so relieved. This freedom allowed us to cut back a bit at work, whereas my brother and sister-in-law are grinding more than ever to pay for three private liberal arts college tuitions. We are now empty nesters spending more time traveling and with each other.

HEALTH SAVINGS ACCOUNTS

Health savings accounts (HSAs) are offered by some employers for those enrolled in a high-deductible health plan. Employees contribute pre-tax dollars and can withdraw them without tax if they are used for qualified medical expenses. HSAs are considered "triple tax-free" because contributions are not taxed (like your 401k contribution), the money grows tax-free, and distributions for qualified medical expenses are not taxed. HSAs are distinguished from a health care flexible spending account in that leftover money in a HSA is carried over and accumulates year after year. After 65 years of age, money can be withdrawn for nonmedical expenses, but it is taxed (similar to your 401k). In 2021 the contribution limit was $3,600 for an individual and $7,200 for a family. The catch-up contribution was $1,000 for those 55 years of age and older.

PEARLS

- If your employer offers a match for your retirement savings, in either a 401k or 403b, contribute at least up to the match when you start your job so you do not leave this "free money" on the table. Increase your annual retirement contribution to the IRS limits as soon as your cash flow allows.

- If your employer offers a Roth 401k, and if you think you will still be in a high tax bracket in retirement, consider switching your retirement account from a traditional to a Roth 401k.

- Contribute to a backdoor Roth IRA annually to the IRS limit to give you another tax-advantaged retirement vehicle and tax diversity in retirement. (Roth IRA withdrawals are not taxed in retirement.)

- If you earn additional income reported on a 1099 (eg, consulting income), open a self-employed 401k instead of a SEP-IRA so you can also participate in the backdoor Roth IRA. Contribute a proportion of your self-employed income (~20%, ask your accountant for the exact figure) to your self-employed 401k annually.

- Open and fund a 529 account for each of your kids to help pay for college and higher education, or even private school expenses before college.

- Contribute to an HSA if offered by your employer.

References

1. Ebeling A. Congress blesses Roth IRAs for everyone, even the well paid. *Forbes.* January 22, 2018. Accessed March 16, 2021. https://www.forbes.com/sites/ashleaebeling/2018/01/22/congress-blesses-roth-iras-for-everyone-even-the-well-paid/?sh=1b83198b7471

2. SEP plan FAQs. Internal Revenue Service. Updated November 10, 2020. Accessed March 16, 2021. https://www.irs.gov/retirement-plans/retirement-plans-faqs-regarding-seps-contributions

3. SEP IRA vs solo 401(k). The White Coat Investor. December 22, 2020. Accessed April 13, 2021. https://www.whitecoatinvestor.com/sep-ira-vs-solo-401k/

4. Trends in college pricing highlights. College Board. Accessed April 26, 2021. https://research.collegeboard.org/trends/college-pricing/highlights

5. Tutorial: the real cost of higher education. Saving for College. Accessed April 17, 2021. https://www.savingforcollege.com/tutorial101/the-real-cost-of-higher-education

6. Flynn K. 529 savings plans and private school tuition. Saving for College. September 28, 2020. Accessed March 16, 2021. https://www.savingforcollege.com/article/529-savings-plans-and-private-school-tuition

7

Taxable Investing

*By periodically investing in an index fund,
the know-nothing investors can actually outperform
most investment professionals.*
—Warren Buffett

Once you exhaust all your tax-advantaged savings vehicles, you have to consider taxable investing. Ultimately, as your income and savings grow, taxable investing may eventually be the largest part of your portfolio. Before taxable investing, it is important to understand the importance of automatic investing, as you will likely do for your 401k, and the associated value of dollar cost averaging.

DOLLAR COST AVERAGING AND LUMP SUM INVESTING

Dollar cost averaging is a smart way to siphon off some of your paycheck to participate in the stock market on a

Shah CP, Sridhar J. *Financial Freedom Rx:
The Physician's Guide to Achieving Financial Independence* (pp 87-100).
© 2021 SLACK Incorporated.

regular basis. The concept is straightforward: you invest the same amount at a set time interval. When the market is up, your dollars buy less; when the market is down, your dollars buy more. This process can be automated by most online brokerages, so that the process is put on autopilot. We would recommend designating a total stock market index fund as your core fund. Ideally, it should be one without a commission (so you do not get charged every time you buy more).

Contrast this strategy with lump sum investing, when one invests a lump sum (hopefully in a diversified manner) at a given point in time. Lump sum investing is great when you have a windfall of money, like an inheritance or a bonus. When investing a large amount of money— or any amount of money—it is important to stick to your asset allocation (see Chapter 8, "Diversification and Asset Allocation") so that you maintain a balanced, well-diversified portfolio.

There are advantages and disadvantages to both dollar cost averaging and lump sum investing. The reality is that you will probably do both, depending on your cash flow. With dollar cost averaging, you gradually invest in the market as you earn a paycheck and thus avoid the possible peril of lump sum investing at the peak of a volatile market. To illustrate, the stock market was very volatile during the 5 years between 2008 and 2013. Figure 7-1 shows that when investing a lump sum at the beginning of 2008, it took 5 years to recover to the initial investment value. When dollar cost averaging in this volatile market, the investor recovered after 2 years and was profitable thereafter to year 5.

The advantages of dollar cost averaging are that it can be automated (easy!), it makes investing less emotional

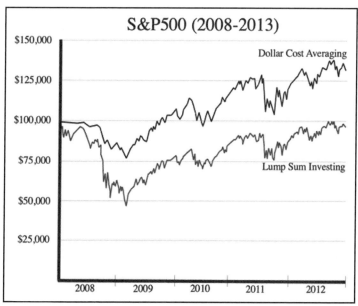

Figure 7-1. During the market volatility between 2008 and 2013, a lump sum investment in 2008 initially lost value and took 5 years to recover. Dollar cost averaging with regular investments during this same period allowed the investor to be profitable. (Reproduced with permission from https://www.millennial-revolution.com/invest/dolla-dolla-dolla-cost -averaging/.)

and stressful, and it smooths out the disturbing losses of recently invested principal in down markets. The mathematics of dollar cost averaging make choppy markets more profitable for investors compared to lump sum investors. Also, because most physicians earn a biweekly or monthly paycheck, dollar cost averaging is the more practical and realistic investment option to invest a proportion of your paycheck before you have time to spend it.

There are two potential drawbacks to dollar cost averaging investing. First, given the frequent purchases, there can be significant transaction costs when dollar cost averaging into funds or assets with purchasing fees. This cost

Figure 7-2. During a period of steady market growth between 1995 and 2000, a lump sum investment in 1995 outperformed dollar cost averaging. (Reproduced with permission from https://www.millennial-revolution .com/invest/dolla-dolla-dolla-cost-averaging/.)

can be eliminated by investing in broad index funds with no transaction fees rather than in individual stocks or other assets carrying commissions. Second, dollar cost averaging is less profitable in an ascending market compared to lump sum investing. For instance, the market rose consistently between 1995 and 2000. As illustrated in Figure 7-2, lump sum investing outperformed dollar cost investing in this well-performing market. Proponents of lump sum investing argue that since the stock market overall tends to increase over time there is a financial advantage to making the single large early purchase. If you have a portfolio diversified over many asset classes, like stocks, bonds, and real estate, you should feel comfortable investing a lump sum as long as you maintain your asset allocation.

How should you start? Assuming you have some money saved and you are already maxing out tax-advantaged retirement accounts, you should use that now for a lump sum investment to get your taxable investing rolling. Then it makes sense to automatically invest in a dollar-cost averaging fashion out of your paycheck to keep your nest egg growing.

My husband and I had maxed out our workplace 403b and individual retirement accounts each year for a number of years and paid off our student debt. Pretty good, right? But for several years we had our excess income accumulating in savings accounts that paid minimal interest. Reaching our retirement goal seemed impossible with such a low interest rate, particularly because it was less than the inflation rate. Something about the term "taxable" investing made us uneasy that investing money outside of our retirement accounts would further increase our tax bill. I was discussing this with a friend, who was shocked at this perception. She explained that with taxable investing one pays capital gains taxes on dividends and on earnings when you sell investments. It does help that the capital gains tax rate is lower than the ordinary income tax rate at my income level. Further, low cost index funds are relatively tax efficient because there is a low turnover rate (not much buying and selling within the fund). If we tax-loss harvested in down markets by exchanging losing lots for a similar index fund, we could bank some losses and actually lower our tax bill. We have been investing our excess savings in a low-cost total stock market index fund and total bond market index fund ever since. Overall, over the years we have outperformed the interest rate of the saving's account at our bank. I just wish we had figured this out many years earlier!

Automatic Investments

To help you save consistently, consider automatic investments from your bank account directly into your brokerage account. It is easy to set up an online account with any brokerage firm of your choice. Two popular ones are Vanguard and Fidelity. They, like others, allow you to invest automatically every week, month, or other interval of your choosing. Whatever amount you specify will magically leave your bank account before you are tempted to spend it. Pay yourself first. This money will work for you as your portfolio grows, whose annual yield may someday eclipse your annual salary. That passive growth does require active discipline early in your career, however.

I completed my residency in 2005 and have been saving and investing ever since. I set up automatic investing between my bank and Vanguard accounts, so that every week some money flows into a total stock market index fund and a municipal bond fund. As my salary increased, I increased the amount of money I automatically invested. And as I grew older,

I would invest a higher proportion of my savings in bonds and less in stocks. This strategy worked well, as the stock market was rising between 2005 and 2008. But then the crash of 2008 happened, and my investment portfolio was slashed in half. It was devastating. My gut wanted to get out of the market and invest in other vehicles. Real estate? Bond ladders? But I just froze and didn't change anything. It turned out that as the market was crashing my automatic investments were buying more index fund and bond shares. I was effectively buying them on sale. A few years later, as the market slowly rebounded, the gains on those cheaper shares really helped bolster my entire portfolio, and I was in the green again and have done great ever since. I've learned to maintain faith in the strategy of so-called dollar cost averaging, which works if you believe the market will gradually increase over time, despite its whims and volatility.

Automatic investing takes the emotion out of investing. As shown in Figure 7-3, human psychology and emotion govern when investors buy and sell. Investors consistently sell when the market is low, when they should be buying, and buy when the market is high, when they should be selling. As busy physicians, putting your investing on autopilot not only allows you to regularly save and invest while dollar cost averaging, but it eliminates the human psychology that may cause you to sell low and buy high.

We frequently see colleagues who save but do not invest because the market is falling (might be an ideal time to invest) or, conversely, because the market is at an all-time high (might be a bad time to invest), resulting in a pile of money in a very low-yield bank savings account. The only hard part for you will be creating and sticking to the plan. We recommend that you take extra hospital calls during bear markets so you don't have time to check the markets and screw up your automatic investing.

The biggest thing that changed the course of my financial life was deleting my stock broker application off my mobile device. My wife and I would invest automatically each pay period, but I would get bored between cases in the operating room and obsessive-compulsively check my accounts to see how they were doing. Anytime I saw a drop I would freak out inside and wonder if I should sell and escape the market. Sometimes I did, and we took a big step backward, doing the classic newbie move of "buying high and selling low." Finally, my wife convinced me to delete the application from my phone, and now I don't check my accounts more than once a week (she's trying to get me down to once a month). I have not made any impulse buy or sells in a while, and my surgery days seem a whole lot less stressful!

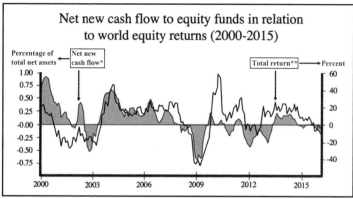

Figure 7-3. Investors tend to buy when the market is up and sell when the market is down. That is the exact opposite of what one should be doing. Human psychology can be the determinant of smart investing. Consider automatic investing to separate emotion and investing. *Net new cash flow = Percentage of previous month-end equity fund assets, as a 6-month moving average. **Total return = Year-over-year percent change in the MSCI All Country World Daily Gross Total Return Index. (This information was collected from the *2016 Investment Company Fact Book*. For the most up-to-date figures about the fund industry, please visit www.icifactbook .org and www.ici.org/research/stats. Reproduced with permission.)

INDEX FUNDS

Most investors, both institutional and individual, will find that the best way to own common stocks is through an index fund that charges minimal fees. Those following this path are sure to beat the net results (after fees and expenses) delivered by the great majority of investment professionals.
—Warren Buffett

Physicians might be smart, but in general we are not smart enough to beat the market consistently. In fact, very few are. Your investment return is possibly the first time in your life that you would be happy to hit the mean, or the average return of the market index. There are many books and articles written about the value of index fund investing

(*The Bogleheads' Guide to Investing, The White Coat Investor, The Elements of Investing*). Index funds are designed to follow a specific index, which might be the total stock market, total bond market, or a sector within the total market. Because index funds are passively managed, they tend to have very low expense ratios, keeping more money in your pocket and low turnovers, making index funds tax efficient. Index fund investing allows you to be diversified across the total market or a sector, depending on the fund.

If you are an experienced investor and have the wherewithal and knowledge to invest in individual stocks, good for you. Selecting successful individual stocks is one strategy that can beat the market, and individual stocks allow for more control of tax events compared to an indexed mutual fund. However, the lack of diversification and associated risk, not to mention the time it takes to remain educated about individual publicly traded companies, makes individual stock investing riskier and less ideal than index funds for the average physician. Stocks require much more knowledge and more diligent oversight than an index fund. Furthermore, the transaction and tax costs of buying and selling stocks can erode gains even if you are able to beat the market over an extended period of time.

You should also avoid high-cost mutual funds with load fees when you first invest and then charge high (> 0.5%) annual expense fees. Do not be lured into a choosing a fund based on its Morningstar rating or past performance. Studies have shown that the top quartile mutual funds over a given 5-year period will on average be evenly distributed in all four quartiles in the next 5-year period. This simply means that past performance is no guarantee of future performance.

Index funds follow the index passively, with low turnover rates, and thus tend to have very low expense ratios.

Remember, in general, the less you pay in expense ratios (fees!), the more you make. Popular index funds include the Vanguard Total Stock Market Index Fund Investor Shares (VTSMX; 0.14% expense ratio), the Vanguard Total Stock Market Index Fund Admiral Shares (VTSAX; $3,000 minimum investment, 0.04% expense ratio), Fidelity Total Market Index Fund (FSKAX; 0.015% expense ratio), and Fidelity ZERO Total Market Index Fund (FZROX; 0% expense ratio). If you have an account through these brokerage firms, there is no transaction cost to buy or sell these index funds, which lend themselves well to automatic investments and dollar cost averaging.

Often, early investors may wish to consider investing excess savings (beyond tax-advantaged retirement and educational accounts) entirely into a total stock market index fund. This fund has more risk and volatility compared to a total bond market fund but has the most potential for growth over one's career. Indeed, the average annual returns were about 8% for total stock market index funds over the past several decades, though there were short-term fluctuations over shorter periods.

TAX-LOSS HARVESTING

Who doesn't love a good sale? It is human nature to be concerned when the market corrects—or crashes—and your portfolio value plummets. Your level of concern may depend on how close you are to retirement. For younger doctors who have less to lose, a big drop in the market allows you to buy shares in your total stock market index fund on sale. For older doctors, whose portfolios have hopefully become more conservative with bonds, market dips also represent an opportunity to buy, or at the very least, stay the course. For all players, market lows are ideal times to tax-loss harvest.

Tax-loss harvesting allows you to capture the loss on individual lots in your taxable portfolio. This loss can be used to offset capital gains, thereby saving on the taxes you otherwise would owe on those gains. Excess harvesting of loss can be carried forward to future years (yes, you will eventually liquidate some or all of your portfolio, likely for gains). And $3,000 of loss can be used against ordinary or dividend income each year.

It is relatively easy to tax-loss harvest when you invest in index funds. For instance, if you own VTSAX and the market is down, identify the lots that are at a loss. You can exchange these specific lots into a very similar index fund, such as the Vanguard 500 Index Fund (VFIAX). In doing so, you harvest the loss and purchase VFIAX at a lower cost basis. Your money continues to be in the game.

For example, if you paid $10,000 for VTSAX and the market dipped 30%, you would sell those lots at $7,000 and harvest $3,000 of loss. You could then immediately purchase $7,000 of VFIAX at a lowered cost basis. The harvested loss can be used to offset $3,000 of your ordinary income (ie, your salary). At a 40% tax bracket, you just saved $1,200 with a few clicks.

There are some important rules with tax-loss harvesting. You cannot exchange into funds that are "substantially identical," even at a different brokerage firm, but you can exchange into highly correlated funds. You cannot repurchase the sold stock or fund for 30 days after the date of sale. Further, you cannot retain any lots of stock or index fund from the 30 days prior to the sale. A purchase during this 61-day period (30 days before, day of sale, and 30 days after) is known as a "wash sale." There are some pitfalls to avoid. If you automatically invest every week, be sure to sell all the lots purchased 30 days prior to your sale date and switch your automatic investments into the new fund. Of note, it is often safer to have your dividends deposited in your account rather than automatically reinvested, so that you do not accidently purchase shares within the 30 days after a sale. Be sure you do not repurchase substantially identical shares in your spouse's account, as these are considered jointly by the Internal Revenue Service. Finally, some states, like New Jersey and Pennsylvania, do not allow losses to be carried forward to future years. Please check the specific rules of your state.

Pearls

- After maximizing tax-advantaged vehicles for retirement and educational savings, consider automatically investing a proportion of your salary before you are tempted to spend it.

- When automatically investing at a regular interval, your dollars will buy more when the market is down and less when the market is up. This so-called dollar cost averaging can allow you to invest consistently and avoid psychological pitfalls even in a volatile market.

- Lump sum investing is when you invest a large amount of money at one time, hopefully into a diversified portfolio.

- Most likely, you will employ both strategies: dollar cost average with your regular paycheck, lump sum investing with bonuses and other windfalls of money.

- Index funds are diversified, inexpensive, and tax-efficient. Consider a total stock market index fund the core holding in your portfolio.

- Tax-loss harvesting is a way to bank paper losses to offset your tax burden while still keeping your money in the game.

8

Diversification and Asset Allocation

I will tell you how to become rich. Close the doors.
Be fearful when others are greedy.
Be greedy when others are fearful.
—Warren Buffett

As we progress in our careers, with less time to recover in the case of a market downturn and with a larger nest egg, most will become more conservative with their investing. This should be done by diversifying your portfolio across many asset classes. Adding asset classes such as bonds, real estate investment trusts (REITs), emerging market stocks, and international stocks to your portfolio can help smooth out the fluctuations of the market. These asset classes are relatively uncoupled (not entirely, in a global market), so the return of one asset class is not necessarily linked to that of another. For instance, as shown in Figure 8-1, real estate was one of the best asset classes in 2006, with a 42% return, while US fixed income was the worst at -4%. However, just 1 year later, real estate was the worst at

Shah CP, Sridhar J. *Financial Freedom Rx:*
The Physician's Guide to Achieving Financial Independence (pp 101-115).
© 2021 SLACK Incorporated.

2007	2008	2009	2010	2011	2012	2013	2014	2015	2016	2017	2018	2019
Emrg Mkt Stocks 39%	US Bonds 5%	Emrg Mkt Stocks 79%	Sm Cap Stocks 27%	US Bonds 8%	Real Estate 28%	Sm Cap Stocks 39%	Real Estate 15%	Lg Cap Stocks 1%	Sm Cap Stocks 21%	Emrg Mkt Stocks 37%	Cash 2%	Lg Cap Stocks 31%
Dev Non-US Stocks 12%	Cash 2%	Real Estate 37%	Real Estate 20%	Lg Cap Stocks 2%	Emrg Mkt Stocks 18%	Lg Cap Stocks 32%	Lg Cap Stocks 14%	US Bonds 1%	Lg Cap Stocks 12%	Dev Non-US Stocks 24%	US Bonds 0%	Sm Cap Stocks 26%
US Bonds 7%	Sm Cap Stocks -24%	Dev Non-US Stocks 34%	Emrg Mkt Stocks 19%	Cash 0%	Dev Non-US Stocks 16%	Dev Non-US Stocks 21%	US Bonds 6%	Cash 0%	Emrg Mkt Stocks 11%	Lg Cap Stocks 22%	Lg Cap Stocks -4%	Dev Non-US Stocks 22%
Lg Cap Stocks 5%	Lg Cap Stocks -37%	Sm Cap Stocks 27%	Lg Cap Stocks 15%	Sm Cap Stocks -4%	Sm Cap Stocks 16%	Real Estate 4%	Sm Cap Stocks 5%	Real Estate -1%	Real Estate 4%	Sm Cap Stocks 15%	Real Estate -6%	Real Estate 22%
Cash 5%	Dev Non-US Stocks -44%	Lg Cap Stocks 26%	Dev Non-US Stocks 9%	Real Estate -6%	Lg Cap Stocks 16%	Cash 0%	Cash 0%	Dev Non-US Stocks -3%	Dev Non-US Stocks 3%	Real Estate 10%	Sm Cap Stocks -11%	Emrg Mkt Stocks 18%
Sm Cap Stocks -2%	Real Estate -48%	US Bonds 6%	US Bonds 7%	Dev Non-US Stocks -12%	US Bonds 4%	US Bonds -2%	Emrg Mkt Stocks -2%	Sm Cap Stocks -4%	US Bonds 3%	US Bonds 4%	Dev Non-US Stocks -14%	US Bonds 9%
Real Estate -7%	Emrg Mkt Stocks -53%	Cash 0%	Cash 0%	Emrg Mkt Stocks -18%	Cash 0%	Emrg Mkt Stocks -3%	Dev Non-US Stocks -4%	Emrg Mkt Stocks -14%	Cash 0%	Cash 1%	Emrg Mkt Stocks -15%	Cash 3%

Figure 8-1. Annual Returns for Key Indices Ranked in Order of Performance (2007–2019). In any given year, performance of different asset classes can vary widely. Particularly as one's investment horizon shortens, it may be worth considering diversifying one's portfolio with different asset classes to stabilize potential volatility. Large Cap Stock (S&P 500) measures the performance of large capitalization US stocks. Small Cap Stock (Russell 2000) measures the performance of small capitalization US stocks. Developed Non-US Stocks (MSCI World ex USA) measure the performance of large and mid-cap equities in Europe, the Middle East, the Pacific region, and Canada. Emerging Market Stocks (MSCI Emerging Markets) measure the performance of equity markets in 26 emerging countries around the world. US Bonds, or Fixed Income (Bloomberg Barclays US Aggregate Bond Index) includes US government, corporate, and mortgage-backed securities with maturities of at least 1 year. Real Estate (FTSE EPRA Nareit Developed REIT Index) measures the stock performance of companies engaged in real estate activities in the North American, European, and Asian real estate markets. Cash (90-day T-bill) is a short-term debt obligation backed by the US Treasury Department. (Reproduced with permission from Callan LLC. https://www.callan.com/.)

-7% while US fixed income returned 7%. Over time, the performance of any single asset class can vary widely, from being one of the best to one of the worst.

Ultimately, your specific investment horizon will help shape your asset allocation. You may have most or all of your assets in stocks, ranging from small to large cap, if you have a 30-year investment horizon. As you progress, and your investment horizon narrows, you might consider adding diversity to your portfolio with other asset classes. Having a diverse portfolio with a blend of different asset classes, like domestic and international stocks, bonds, real estate, and cash, allows your portfolio to grow with less volatility.

WHAT SHOULD MY ASSET ALLOCATION BE?

For most physician investors, keeping asset allocation simple with a balance of stocks and bonds is sufficient when beginning to build wealth. One can further diversify as one's portfolio grows. At the start of one's career, with a lifetime of earning ahead (not to mention time to recover from down markets), it is reasonable to be heavily weighted in stocks. For those in their 30s, a sample portfolio might include 90% in a total stock market index fund and 10% in bonds. Over time, one should consider becoming more conservative and protecting oneself from downside risk by increasing one's bond allocation. Remember, bonds are boring, usually keeping up with inflation, but they experience lower volatility and are not prone to the sometimes violent swings of the stock market. And as your portfolio grows, you slowly shift from trying to win more to trying not to lose what you have. There are several opinions on the ideal ratio of stocks:bonds based on your stage in life. One popular rule is 100 minus your age equals the recommended percentage allocation in stocks, with the remaining percentage assigned to bonds. For example, a 30-year-old physician would have a 70/30 stock-to-bond ratio. However, physicians begin making the meat of their income later in life, and as a result many choose to be more aggressive than the 100 minus age rule. Thus, for those in their 40s, a reasonable stock-to-bond ratio might be 80:20. And for those in their 60s, the balance might be 50:50. Regardless of where you start, your allocation toward bonds can and probably should increase by 10% to 20% every decade of life, thereby making your overall taxable portfolio more conservative and more secure as you approach retirement. Keep in mind that there is no universal prescription for asset allocation. It depends on many factors, including your age, net worth, risk tolerance, earning potential, and investment horizon. You can determine the optimal ratio for you. It is something for you to decide for yourself, possibly with the input of a financial advisor if needed (see Chapter 10).

There are several ways you can integrate bonds into your portfolio. The simplest and most liquid means would be to purchase bond index funds in your brokerage account, just as you would purchase stock index funds. From a practical perspective, if you are already automatically investing, you can allocate a larger percentage of your portfolio toward a bond index fund. Assuming you are still working and earning a regular income, rebalancing the allocation of your automatic investments obviates the need to sell some of your stock index funds to buy bond index funds. Thus, in your taxable accounts you avoid a taxable event. Of course, in your tax-advantaged accounts, like your 401k, you can sell and rebalance without tax implications.

There are many total bond index funds from which you can choose. Options include Vanguard Total Bond Market Index Fund Investor Shares (VBMFX; 0.15% ratio), Vanguard Total Bond Market Index Fund Admiral Shares (VBTLX; $3,000 minimum, 0.05% expense ratio), Fidelity Total Bond Fund (FTBFX; 0.45% expense ratio), and Fidelity US Bond Index Fund (FXNAX; 0.025% expense ratio).

It is worth doing your homework when deciding upon your bond exposure. Though total bond index funds are inexpensive, diversified, and liquid, they tend to have low yields. It is worth considering municipal bond funds that are federal income tax free, and possibly state tax income free as well, depending on the fund and your state of residence. Of course, tax-free dividends leave much more money in your pocket (or in your portfolio) compared to taxable dividends. A few national municipal bond funds are Fidelity Intermediate Municipal Income Fund (FLTMX; 0.37% expense ratio), Fidelity Municipal Income Fund (FHIGX; 0.46% expense ratio), Fidelity Municipal Bond Index Fund (FMBIX; 0.07% expense ratio), Vanguard Intermediate-Term Tax-Exempt Fund Investor Shares (VWITX; 0.17% expense ratio), and Vanguard Intermediate-Term Tax-Exempt Fund Admiral Shares (VWIUX; 0.09% expense ratio, $50,000 minimum). Though no guarantee of future performance, it is worth comparing the past and current performance of these funds and others online, using websites such as Google Finance or Yahoo Finance. For example, both Vanguard and Fidelity have a Massachusetts municipal bond fund, which is particularly attractive to high-earning Massachusetts state residents. The dividends from each of these funds are exempt from federal and state tax, and thus provide fixed, tax-free income. The Vanguard Massachusetts

Tax-Exempt Fund (VMATX) has an expense ratio of 0.13% and a distribution yield of 2.83%. The Fidelity Massachusetts Municipal Income Fund (FDMMX) has an expense ratio of 0.46% and a distribution yield of 2.57%. The 5-year return as of December 31, 2019, was 0.73% for Vanguard's fund, compared to -2.20% for Fidelity's. Though both funds are competitive and offer tax-free fixed income, the Vanguard fund is more attractive given its lower expense ratio, higher dividend, and greater appreciation.

Bond funds, especially funds that hold longer-term bonds, can lose money when interest rates rise. In comparison, individual bonds are redeemed for full value if held to their maturity. As you progress in your career, it may be worth considering bond ladders rather than bond funds. Bond ladders involve purchasing individual bonds that mature at different times, hence the "ladder." If these bonds are held until maturity, and if the underlying holding does not default on the bond, your principal will be returned to you. And while you hold the bond, you will be paid a dividend. Bond ladders are a good way of earning passive fixed income in a relatively conservative manner. However, the bonds are not immediately liquid, as ideally you should hold them until maturity. You can sell them prematurely, but often at a cost. From a practical perspective, you can purchase bond ladders from a financial planner, or if you have the wherewithal you can create and purchase one using an online brokerage like Fidelity.

Remember that your asset allocation should be calculated for your entire portfolio, including retirement and taxable accounts together rather than within each individual vehicle. It makes sense to weight more of one class of assets in one account than another. For example, stocks tend to be more tax advantaged than bonds (with the exception of municipal bonds), so you should optimally choose to keep of all your bond funds and bond ladders in retirement accounts to maximize your tax efficiency. On the other hand, international stock funds may qualify you for a foreign tax credit on your income taxes come April. These funds are better placed in your taxable accounts to improve tax efficiency.

Starting off with my investments at age 32, I allocated 100% of my investments in stocks. The market did great, and so did my portfolio as my automatic investments continued to grow. In my mid-40s I got greedy and chose to keep my 100% stock allocation, figuring more of a good thing could only get me to a retirement by age 50 faster. Then the 2008 market crash happened, and retirement seemed a whole lot farther away. I'm retired now, but since the crash have kept a much more conservative mix of stocks/bonds. Now, even with the market at all-time highs, I am 75/25 bonds to stocks and looking to increase that ratio in my retirement years to keep my portfolio whole and less volatile.

REBALANCING

Rebalancing is simply forcing yourself to buy low and sell high. Perhaps once or twice a year, especially if the market has risen or fallen significantly, it makes sense to log into your brokerage account and determine your proportion of stocks to bonds. Put a reminder in your phone to do this.

Table 8-1		
ANNUAL RETURNS FOR KEY INDICES RANKED IN ORDER OF PERFORMANCE (2007–2019)		
AGE (YEARS)	STOCK ALLOCATION	BOND ALLOCATION
20–29	100%	0%
30–39	90%–100%	0%–10%
40–49	70%–80%	20%–30%
50–59	60%–70%	30%–40%
60–69	40%–60%	40%–60%
70+	<40%	>60%

It keeps things very simple if you only have two funds in your account! If your predetermined ratio were to have 10% bonds and 90% stocks, and one of those funds outperformed the other, you could rebalance to maintain the 10% bond to 90% stock ratio. There are no tax implications if you make these adjustments in a retirement account like your 401k. In a taxable account, there are a few ways to do this without selling and paying taxes; you can employ one, two, or all three of these strategies. If you have excess cash on the sidelines, you can buy more of the fund that is underperforming to rebalance your ratio. You can adjust your automatic investments for the next few months to adjust these ratios. Or, you can transfer some funds from of the overperforming fund into the underperforming fund; this would trigger a taxable event if you sold at a gain (in a taxable account only). As mentioned previously, one can also use tax-loss harvesting to offset any taxable events incurred during this process.

Table 8-1 serves as a rough guide for those wishing to have a simple two-fund portfolio (total stock index and total bond index).

OTHER ALLOCATIONS WORTH CONSIDERING

Of course, there are many other asset classes outside of stocks and bonds. You do not need to invest in all of them, or even any of them. If you have done the things discussed so far (determined a budget, purchased appropriate insurances, paid down debt, maximized workplace savings, and maintained a simple two-fund portfolio), you are already on track to winning the game.

As your portfolio continues to grow, however, it may be worth diversifying further with real estate and international and emerging market stocks. (There are a host of other asset classes, like private equity and commodities, that are likely beyond the scope of most of our readers.)

There are several ways to invest in real estate, ranging from actively buying and renting apartments to passively holding REITs. Many index funds have a small component of REIT investment as well. If you have the time and energy to purchase and rent real estate, that can be a lucrative means of regular income while you hopefully enjoy capital appreciation on your properties. Several good resources on real estate investing worth reading if you wish to pursue such an investment are listed in Appendix B.

REITs represent a more passive way to dabble in real estate without the work of owning your own properties. A REIT is a real estate investment trust that pools money from investors in particular real estate investments. You can purchase shares of public REITs in your brokerage account to gain exposure to specific property types, from multifamily to retail to industrial. Keep in mind that dividends from REITs are taxed as ordinary income, unlike C-Corp dividends from a typical stock that are taxed at the more favorable capital gains tax. Thus, REIT dividends are tax inefficient for high earners like physicians if kept in a taxable account. REITs are better for tax-deferred accounts for high earners. Also, remember that REITs are included in many broad index funds. For example, the Vanguard Total Stock Market Index Fund (VTSM) has 1.72% of its investment in REITs. One could invest directly in a REIT or a real estate index fund to increase one's exposure.

As an alternative to REITs, you can invest in a real estate index fund, such as the Fidelity Real Estate Index Fund (FSRNX, expense ratio 0.07%) or the Vanguard Real Estate Index Fund (VGSIX, expense ratio 0.26%). These are broadly diversified funds that give you exposure to real estate with a modest dividend and, hopefully, growth over time.

It is reasonable to include only a domestic stock index fund in your portfolio, particularly since so many domestic companies have a global foothold. The S&P 500 is already a global index, with a significant chunk of its sales derived from an international market (29% in 2019).[1] Further, most emerging market funds and international funds give you outsized exposure to often relatively poorly positioned regional companies (like nationally focused banks and oil companies) rather than world-leading global firms like Amazon, which you find in the S&P 500. Finally, shareholder rights are typically better in the United States.

On the other hand, while some investors might choose, rationally, to avoid international investing, others may wish to diversify a sliver of their stock allocation toward international and emerging markets. For instance, if you hold 70% of your portfolio in stocks, you could consider allocating 50% to 60% toward a total domestic stock market index fund, and 5% to 10% toward, each, an international and emerging markets index fund. Examples of international stock market index funds include Vanguard Total International Stock Index Fund (VGTSX; expense ratio 0.17%) and Fidelity International Index Fund (FSPSX; expense ratio 0.035%). Examples of emerging market index funds include Vanguard Emerging Markets Stock Index Fund (VEIEX; expense ratio 0.14%) and Fidelity Emerging Markets Index Fund (FPADX; expense ratio 0.08%). As with bond index funds, it may be worth doing some homework here, as there are relatively low-cost actively managed international and emerging market sector funds that might outperform total market index funds in this space.

HELP ME ALLOCATE MY ASSETS!

Lifecycle Funds

If you do not wish to manage your asset allocation yourself, many brokerage firms offer diverse funds for targeted retirement dates. For example, based on your age, you may target a retirement date of 2040 and invest in a lifecycle fund such as the Vanguard Target Retirement 2040 Fund (VFORX). These lifecycle funds are weighted more heavily with equities early on and gradually reduce equity exposure and increase bond exposure as the retirement date nears. To illustrate, the VFORX has the following makeup as of September 2019:

- Vanguard Total Market Stock Index Fund 50.4%
- Vanguard Total International Stock Index Fund 33.0%
- Vanguard Total Bond Market II Index Fund 11.5%
- Vanguard Total International Bond Index Fund 5.1%

Lifecycle funds are a great option for those who want to "set it and forget it" for a low expense ratio (0.14% for VFORX).

LifeStrategy Funds

While lifecycle funds get more conservative as your approach retirement age, Vanguard has LifeStrategy funds that maintain a specific balance between stocks and bonds by automatically rebalancing. There are four options, depending on your risk tolerance, ranging from 20% stocks and 80% bonds to 80% stocks and 20% bonds. The expense ratio is low at 0.13%. This is a good option if you wish to maintain a constant asset allocation.

Robo Investors

There are an emerging number of "robo investors" options, such as Wealthfront, Betterment, Personal Capital, and Schwab Intelligent Portfolios, that offer relatively inexpensive wealth management services online. They operate under the same principles as this book, by investing your money in a globally diversified portfolio of low-cost index funds. Further, they help reduce your tax burden by tax-loss harvesting in down markets. Betterment and Wealthfront charge a 0.25% management fee, which is typically cheaper than the average financial planner (who may charge about 1% of assets under management). These robo investors are a good and relatively inexpensive way to create and maintain a diversified portfolio. This is a good option for someone who does not want to manage their own portfolio, but also does not want to pay a 1% fee to a financial advisor.

WHERE SHOULD I PLACE VARIOUS ASSETS TO MAXIMIZE AFTER-TAX RETURN?

It is important to remember the tax implications of individual investments. Some investment dividends are tax-free and can be smartly held in a taxable account, while other investment dividends are taxed as ordinary income and should be held in a tax-deferred account if possible.

For instance, municipal bond funds issued within one's state yield dividends that are free from federal and state taxes. Such municipal bond funds can be held in a taxable account without any tax implications and are a good fixed income stream. To the contrary, dividends payments from most REITs are taxed as ordinary income at the shareholder's top marginal tax rate. This can reduce dividends by nearly half for earners in the top income bracket in high-tax states. Thus, REIT dividends are tax inefficient and should be held in a tax-deferred account, like a 401k or Roth individual retirement account.

Most dividends are "qualified dividends," and are taxed at the more favorable capital tax rate. High-yield bonds, for example, can pay reasonable dividends but are subject to capital gains tax. For those whose financial goal is growth, it is important to minimize the drag that taxes have on dividend earnings, which are often reinvested. This is another reason index funds are attractive for taxable investment accounts. Index funds tend to have low turnover, meaning less buying and selling, and thus trigger fewer taxable events and are tax efficient.

Figure 8-2 ranks the various funds we have discussed from the most tax-efficient to the least. Consider placing the least tax-efficient funds in a tax-advantaged account if possible. Remember, one's overall portfolio is

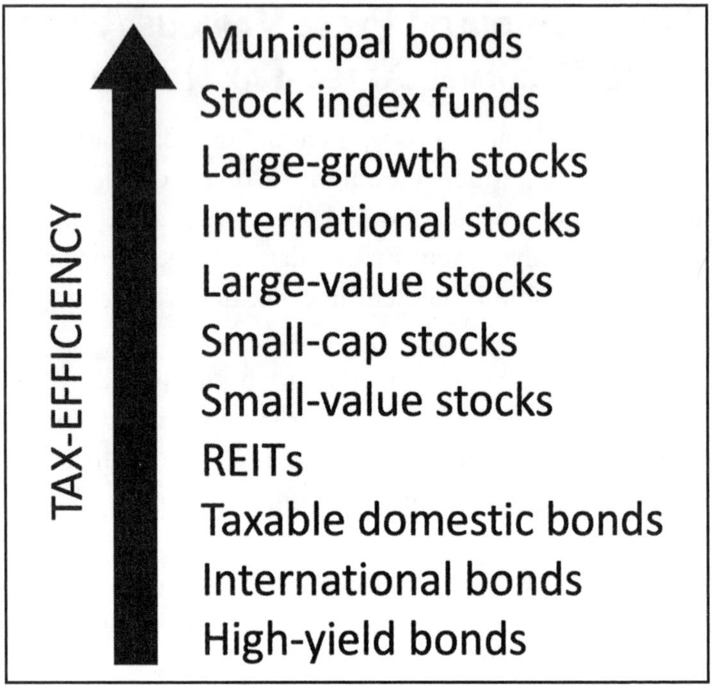

Figure 8-2. Asset classes vary in their tax-efficiency, with high-yield bonds being the least tax-efficient, and municipal bonds being the most tax-efficient.

the totality of their taxable, tax-deferred, and tax-free accounts. Allocation of funds between these accounts to maximize after-tax returns can be as important as one's overall asset allocation.

PEARLS

- In the long run, it is important to maintain a diversified portfolio, not just across time with dollar cost averaging, but across various asset classes like stocks and bonds (and maybe real estate, international stocks, and emerging market stocks).

- Remember that your asset allocation is determined by lumping all of your assets across accounts rather than within individual accounts.

- Consider index funds, or low-cost actively managed municipal bond funds, for your bond exposure.

- Consider bond ladders, perhaps even municipal bond ladders, to provide some fixed income and bond exposure as you get older, so long as you do not need liquidity.

- As you get older, consider rebalancing your portfolio to become more conservative, pulling away from stocks, which may be more volatile, and toward bonds, which are typically more stable.

- Consider a lifecycle fund, LifeStrategy fund, or robo investing, if you wish to pay a small premium to have someone maintain a balanced portfolio for you.

- Place tax-efficient funds, like municipal bond funds (preferably issued within your state) or stock index funds, in taxable accounts.

- Place funds that are less tax-efficient, like REITs or high-yield bonds, in a tax-deferred account like a 401k.

REFERENCE

1. Bacani EL. S&P 500 companies' non-US revenue share hits 10-year low–Goldman Sachs. S&P Global. Accessed April 26, 2021. https://www.spglobal.com/marke-tintelligence/en/news-insights/latest-news-headlines/s-p-500-companies-non-us-revenue-share-hits-10-year-low-8211-goldman-sachs-59094991

9

Defense Part 2
Life, Homeowners, and Umbrella Insurance

The only defense against the world is a thorough knowledge of it.
—John Locke

Assuming that you do not suffer from major lifestyle creep with rapidly expanding expenses, you will eventually get to a point when wealth preservation becomes more important than growing wealth. We discussed the importance of defense in Chapter 4, specifically with the two insurances that are critical to establish early in one's career, namely disability and malpractice insurance. (We included health insurance, but hopefully you have had continuous coverage your whole life.)

As you progress through your career and life, other insurances become important. Herein we will briefly discuss life, homeowners, and umbrella insurance.

Shah CP, Sridhar J. *Financial Freedom Rx:*
The Physician's Guide to Achieving Financial Independence (pp 117-122).
© 2021 SLACK Incorporated.

LIFE INSURANCE

Life insurance protects your spouse and other loved ones against your death with a lump sum post-tax payment. Consider term life insurance, which avoids the costs and complexity of whole life insurance and other similar policies that tie investments into your life insurance. Term life insurance is typically inexpensive for a younger physician. To keep it simple, plan on buying a term life insurance policy at young age once you are married and/or have dependents. Consider a policy large enough to cover, at minimum, such expenses as your home mortgage and college tuition for your kids in case of your untimely death. Buy level-premium insurance, meaning that your premium payments stay fixed over time. Consider buying a long-term policy, such as 30 years, to cover you into your older years. You can drop the policy later in life once you no longer need coverage as you "self-insure" with your own savings.

How much life insurance you buy depends on your family situation, but generally the bare minimum for a physician with a family would be $1,000,000, and the maximum would be somewhere in the neighborhood of $5,000,000. One strategy to decrease your life insurance coverage as you progress toward financial independence is to buy separate policies with different terms. For example, if you had a goal of $3,000,000 you could purchase three separate $1,000,000 policies with terms of 10, 20, and 30 years, respectively. Your total premium costs would decrease every 10 years. In terms of coverage, if you were to pass away within the first 10 years, your heirs would receive $3,000,000. If you passed in 25 years, after you had 25 years of earnings and savings, your heirs would still receive $1,000,000, plus your estate. The rationale for this strategy is that, the longer you live and earn, the closer to financial independence you should be, and the less life insurance coverage you should need.

It is worth mentioning that there will be plenty of people who will try to sell you whole life insurance. Be very wary. These policies are designed to be sold and not bought, with significant embedded fees. If you wish to consider a whole life insurance policy, please read and understand the fine print, and consider seeking an unbiased opinion from a neutral financial planner or lawyer.

Homeowners Insurance

Homeowners insurance protects your property in the case of damage. If you have a home, you should have a good policy to protect your asset. There are different types of coverage depending on geography; for example, in Florida separate flood insurance is usually purchased and not covered in a typical policy. The same may apply for specific insurance to cover damages from a natural disaster, such as hurricane insurance. There are three important points with homeowners insurance. First, you should absolutely have it if you own your domicile. Unfortunately, most people do not fully protect their homes. The majority of US homes, 67%, are underinsured, and the typical under-insurance amount is 22%.[1] Second, insure your property at replacement cost, not actual cash value. Replacement cost covers the full replacement cost of your house, whereas actual value pays only the depreciated value. Replacement cost insurance is more expensive, but worth the increased premium as it ensures that one has enough money to cover the replacement cost of one's belongings and house in the event of damage or loss. Third, try and obtain guaranteed replacement cost in your policy; this will put your house back together as it was before the damage regardless of cost, even if it exceeds policy limits, protecting the homeowner from sudden increases in construction costs. Guaranteed replacement cost coverage is worth investigating if it is a feasible option that fits within your budget.

Be sure to ask your insurance agent if you are eligible for any discounts. For example, if you live in a hurricane-prone region, getting a wind mitigation survey to prove that you have impact windows could help reduce your annual premium cost.

UMBRELLA INSURANCE

Umbrella insurance is extra liability insurance that shields you from liability expenses beyond what your specific policies may cover. For example, if you have car insurance, your insurance may cover up to a certain maximum amount of liability incurred during an accident. An umbrella policy would then pick up any liability beyond that to the limit of your policy in an effort to protect your personal assets. Umbrella insurances require you to max out your other insurances and typically are inexpensive. If you are just starting your career and have few assets, you might not yet need an umbrella policy, but as your assets grow, your exposure to liability will inevitably grow as well. Thus, for high-earning professionals moving up in the world, purchasing an umbrella policy at a level to cover your assets is a wise investment. Remember that umbrella insurance covers personal liability, which includes any damages that result from unfortunate but not uncommon events such as car accidents. It also would cover you in case of suits for libel, slander, or injury on properties you may own (if you do end up as a renting landlord or with workers at your home). Of note, umbrella insurance does not play any role in professional liability, and would not be part of the equation in a malpractice suit, for example.

> Our au pair got in a car accident with our car. She wasn't hurt (and our kids were not in the car), but the other driver was injured. It's a complicated story, but because our au pair was insured through our car insurance, we were liable for the damage to both cars and for the other driver's injuries. Thank God we had additional liability coverage with our umbrella insurance. It was more than enough to protect our assets while appropriately compensating the other driver.

PEARLS

- Get term life insurance when you have assets (eg, house) and/or responsibilities (eg, spouse, kids). Consider layering several policies so you have a decreasing ladder of coverage as you progress throughout your career.

- Avoid whole life insurance policies due to the high fees often associated with such policies.

- Purchase adequate homeowners insurance, preferably at guaranteed replacement cost of your property.

- Umbrella insurance is a cheap way to maximize your personal liability insurance to cover the value of your estate.

REFERENCE

1. Underinsurance: is your home covered for all it's worth? Nationwide. Accessed March   16,   2021.   https://www.nationwide.com/lc/resources/home/articles/ underinsurance

10

Financial Advisors

Most people don't plan to fail, they fail to plan.
—John Beckley

As busy professionals with growing bank accounts, physicians often find it more time efficient to outsource various components of their lives, such as lawn maintenance and housecleaning services. The same temptation exists for financial planning. Indeed, a trusted financial advisor can be extremely beneficial for many physicians who do not have the time, interest, or knowledge for managing their finances. It is certainly better for many physicians to pay someone 1% of their assets to appropriately manage their wealth than it would be to have a chunk of money sitting in a low-interest bank account depreciating with inflation. However, what about you? You took the time and effort to read this book, suggesting that you have interest in and knowledge about your personal finances. Would

Shah CP, Sridhar J. *Financial Freedom Rx:*
The Physician's Guide to Achieving Financial Independence (pp 123-135).
© 2021 SLACK Incorporated.

you benefit from a financial advisor? Possibly. There are instances when hiring a financial planner makes sense to help manage either all or a portion of your portfolio.

WHEN DOES HIRING A
FINANCIAL ADVISOR MAKE SENSE?

Ultimately, having a financial plan is the most essential component in achieving financial independence. If you simply do not have the time or bandwidth to learn the basics that go into successful planning, hiring an ethical financial advisor can be very helpful to evaluate and craft your overall financial plan. You can determine how many services, or how few, they offer you. They can ensure that you have the appropriate insurances in place and are maximizing tax-advantaged investment vehicles and help manage your taxable portfolio. If your alternative is stockpiling cash in a low-interest savings account while grinding away at work, consider hiring a financial advisor. A financial advisor can be helpful in diversifying your portfolio with a blend of stocks and bonds, as well as alternative investments such as real estate investment trusts (REITs) and private equity funds. Further, if you are unable to resist the emotional pulls compelling you to sell in market downturns and buy during bull markets, a financial planner can help you take the emotion out of investing. They should handle necessary tasks for portfolio management, such as rebalancing and tax-loss harvesting. If you tend to be attracted to dangerously speculative investments, a good financial manager should steer you away from risky options and toward better, more stable ones.

You do not have to use a financial advisor for your entire portfolio. Many people are capable of doing the tasks outlined in this guidebook: making a budget, getting appropriate insurances, paying down debt, maximizing tax-advantaged accounts, and investing surplus income automatically into a total stock market index fund and municipal bond fund at a fixed interval. If you can do all that, you can stop there! But you can consider utilizing a financial planner just for alternative investments and for financial advice as questions arise. For instance, you might consider investing a small proportion of your portfolio, say 10% to 20%, with a financial advisor to help diversify a growing portfolio. They can help you buy municipal and/or corporate bond ladders, individual REITs, and possibly private equity funds. If you are interested in these specific types of illiquid assets, they might be harder (or impossible) to purchase with your online brokerage firm. However, you certainly do not need to complicate your portfolio further with such investments, so please consider this completely optional.

How to Hire a Financial Manager

Much like finding a good surgeon to replace your or a family member's knee, finding a good financial manager can feel like an impossible task given the wealth of options (many of them are not so scrupulous). It is often helpful to get recommendations from your colleagues who have had a good experience with their financial manager. This is often the best place to start. Here is a core list of factors to consider in choosing a potential advisor prior to hiring them.

First, understand what specifically you want your financial manager to do. Types of managers include investment advisors, retirement planners, and financial planners. Investment advisors focus exclusively on your portfolio, while retirement planners can help navigate investments, pensions, and Social Security to ensure that your retirement income is tax-efficient and steady. Financial planners can assist with investments and retirement, but also can aid with savings calculations and insurances.

Next, get a sense of what your manager will cost. Financial advisors can make income via an annual flat fee, by commission, as an annual fee calculated as a percentage of the assets they manage (assets under management [AUM]), by the hour, or a combination of any of the above. In general, if you are able to avoid commission-based advisors, you will reduce costs and conflict of interest. Commission-based advisors are incentivized to sell you products that make them money, hence the conflict. For instance, if a potential advisor is pushing whole life insurance, a product designed to be sold and not purchased, turn and run the other way. Fee-only advisors cannot accept commissions or kickbacks from their company and theoretically may offer more unbiased counsel. Though flat annual fees or hourly fees are often the more cost-effective than commission-based service, not all services may be covered with your base fee. It is important to understand the cost of additional transactions. You might have to negotiate to ensure that services such as tax preparation and insurance underwriting can be included at reduced cost, if these services are even offered by your financial advisor.

During residency, we were introduced to a gentleman who helped residents get better rates on disability insurance. Like many of my colleagues, I utilized his services to underwrite my disability policy; he seemed reasonable and capable, so when he offered to take care of my financial investments as an attending, I went for it. Little did I know that he was a commission-based advisor who was going to nickel-and-dime me for the next 5 years with multiple small transactions spread throughout the year. The crazy thing is that I was so busy building my practice and worrying about my day-to-day finances that I didn't even notice that my big-picture financials were getting messy. I would get annual financial reports, but they seemed like gibberish to me, and I figured that, since my nest egg was getting bigger, he must be doing pretty well. What finally tipped me off was when the market dropped and my nest egg went down for the first time. I went through the reports with a fine-toothed comb and realized what he was doing and how much money I was leaving on the table for him each year. I dropped him as an advisor and moved all my assets to low-cost passive index funds at Fidelity. Looking back, it was my own fault for not asking the right questions of the advisor before employing him. He didn't even have any credentials to justify his position as an advisor! It would be akin to a patient signing up for a cardiac ablation procedure with me and not knowing if I had an MD or not. I do not think all financial advisors are bad, but I would just be cautious.

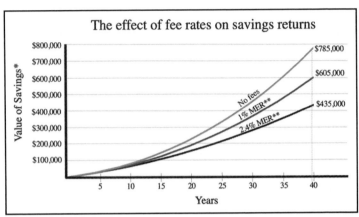

Figure 10-1. As the management expense ratio (MER) increases from 0% to 1% to 2.4%, there is a significant reduction in the value of one's portfolio. The lesson is to keep management fees as low as possible to retain more money in one's portfolio. *Annual rate of return = 5%, **MER = management expense ratio. (Adapted from C. D. Howe Institute, 2014 Ontario budget papers.)

Advisors who charge a certain percentage of your AUM often require that you already have a relatively large portfolio. This management fee is often around 1% but does vary (eg, Vanguard's is 0.3%). Your advisor might charge a smaller percentage of your AUM as your portfolio grows. Of course, as your portfolio grows your absolute costs will steadily increase. This can get expensive over the life of your portfolio, but if your advisor is helping you grow a diverse and tax-efficient portfolio, it may be worth the costs, especially if the alternative is to stash money under your mattress (Figure 10-1).

Remember that a financial manager ultimately is working for you. not out of benevolence, but as an employee who is receiving payment either directly or via expenses. Still, some (but not all!) financial advisors have a fiduciary requirement. This means that they are legally obligated to make financial decisions based on your interests. Always stick to advisors who carry such a requirement. Also, try and find advisors who have had experience working with physicians and understand the unique parts of our profession, such as physician student loan forgiveness and medical contracts.

As you would with any other person you would hire, do your homework on a financial advisor before signing up. This includes reviewing their professional designations to make sure the credentials line up with the advertising. Ideally your advisor should be a Chartered Financial Analyst (CFA), a Certified Financial Planner (CFP), and/or a Chartered Financial Consultant (ChFC). You can perform an online search to ensure that your potential manager has had no prior untoward incidents or legal actions. Ask for references and contacts with current clients so you can get a frank assessment of your potential advisor's style and execution.

One title you may encounter is Chartered Life Underwriter (CLU). CLUs have expertise in life insurance and estate planning. They typically receive a commission for selling insurance and thus can be incentivized to sell high-priced policies. It is important to understand potential conflicts of interest, particularly when an advisor is trying to sell you something. Always maintain a healthy level of skepticism if someone is sitting on the opposite side of the table as a salesperson rather than sitting next to you as your advocate.

Before you hire an advisor, it can be helpful to get a sense of what your investment plan may look like. Feel free to ask for sample portfolios of current clients and review presented options for any oddly out of place high-expense funds. Believe it or not, many advisors are not used to being asked for a philosophy or plan, and it is a red flag if it seems like they plan to just "wing it." Also ask where

investments will be stationed. Sound, honest advisors will
have a policy of ensuring that your portfolio is actually
under a separate, third-party company (typically one of
the large investment firms). That way, while your advisor has access to make transactions within your portfolio,
you as the client will receive unbiased statements from the
third-party company, minimizing conflict of interest in re-
porting performance.

Overseeing a Financial Manager

Financial managers, like any other employee, require
supervision. A critical point to address when starting a
relationship is how often and in what manner you will
communicate. It can be too easy to hire an advisor and
then have your bank account become passive income for
the advisor. Whether it is via email, phone conferences, or
face-to-face lunches, maintain a relationship with your advisor, both to get updates on your progress and to remind
them that you are paying attention. It is crucial that you
continue to maintain your financial education so you can
make informed decisions along with your advisor. There
may be instances when a financial advisor's conflict of
interest might bias their recommendation. For example,
they might suggest a financial instrument with high fees,
like whole life insurance, which an informed client should
be able to critically evaluate.

Every personal financial plan drawn up by a professional financial planner should receive a second opinion
from one's accountant. Further, the plan should be deeply
understood by both the physician and their spouse. You
should expect to receive statements at consistent intervals.
Review all reports and keep tabs on expenses. Feel free to

ask your advisor for a periodic breakdown of expenses in both absolute and percentage terms. If there seem to be an excess number of transactions, be careful and remember that many advisors are paid based on commission per transaction. Do not be afraid to politely but bluntly ask why certain transactions were necessary; after all, it is your bankroll that is funding the whole enterprise.

How You Can Get Fleeced by Financial Managers

Managers can win the game for themselves and pull physicians back in one of three major ways:

1. By being paid an annual fee (whether flat or percentage of total assets managed) and then doing no managing. Inaction is easy passive income for the advisor at the expense of the client.

2. By maximizing commissions with more frequent than necessary sales. Small, seemingly innocent but unnecessary transactions add up across clients and allow an unscrupulous manager to compound small profits.

3. By pushing high-cost policies that should not necessarily be part of a prudent financial plan. Two common pushes from managers are whole life insurance policies and high-cost variable or indexed annuities.

Whole life insurance provides a death benefit for your heirs while also accumulating a cash value within the policy that you can access if needed during your life. Unlike term life insurance, whole life insurance does not expire after a certain term, assuming you continue to pay your premiums. However, whole life insurance policies carry expensive up-front administrative fees and agent commissions, contributing to premiums that cost several-fold more than typical premiums for term life insurance. Unfortunately, in many cases whole life insurance policies are written for the benefit of the seller rather than the purchaser.

Another potentially high-cost instrument is a variable or indexed annuity. Annuities are contracts purchased from an insurance company where one either pays a lump sum or several payments and then receives fixed distributions either immediately or at a deferred time. Annuities essentially allow the consumer to create their own pension plan, either for a prespecified amount of time or for life. Your balance grows tax-free, but the disbursements are taxed as ordinary income, not at the more favorable capital gains tax rate. There are three types of annuities: fixed, variable, and indexed. Fixed annuities pay a guaranteed amount with a low interest rate. Variable annuities are invested in mutual funds, and the retirement payments are based on the performance of these funds. Indexed annuities have a guaranteed minimum payout, but some degree of it is tied to the market index. Many variable and indexed annuities carry high fees that benefit the seller (your advisor) and, in general, are not recommended.

Keep in mind that there are some benefits to annuities, including protection from creditors in some states and exclusion from college financial aid assessments. Further, a fixed single premium immediate annuity (SPIA) might be advisable for those who think they will outlive their money in retirement. For an SPIA, one pays a lump sum premium to receive a fixed immediate annuity.

How You Can Be Enriched by a Financial Advisor

A good, trustworthy financial advisor can be hard to find but can greatly reduce the stress of creating and managing your financial plan. Ultimately, deciding whether to hire one is as personal a decision as deciding whether you cut your own grass versus hiring a landscaping service (with much larger fiscal implications!). Do some honest self-reflection and understand that, even if you do hire an advisor, it is still very important to know financial basics so that you can critically evaluate your advisor's performance.

I think that in the do-it-yourself investment community financial advisors have gotten a bad reputation, maybe for good reason because of the few bad eggs out there. However, I also think a good advisor is worth their weight in gold once you reach a certain stage in your life as a physician. When I was 35, unmarried, and working one job, doing my own finances and taxes was easy and minimally time-consuming. Now, at 55, I would have to juggle the finances of my marriage (and subsequent divorce), my investment plan, my taxes, my kids' educational future, my eventual retirement, and how my practice and property ownership factors into all of this in the big picture. It would be impossible for me to do this alone, and I am much happier having someone trustworthy guide me through the complexities rather than spending my free weekends doing a less-than-optimal job of learning how to do it myself. I found a financial quarterback who came highly recommended, has credentials, charges a flat fee, and communicates with me on a monthly basis to update me on the progress of my investments (and taxes when the season comes). So, yes, you do not need a financial advisor, but then again, do you need a plumber to fix your toilet when it leaks? For me it's a peace of mind and quality of life issue.

PEARLS

- A financial advisor can be an important partner and maintain your financial plan.
- Financial advisors make money by different reimbursement models, which in turn impact their degree of conflict of interest. These models include: annual flat fee, hourly fee, commission, a percentage of AUM, or a combination. In general, an annual or hourly fee reduces conflict of interest and might save you money compared to paying a percentage of your (growing) AUM.
- Having a financial advisor manage your wealth in a diversified and tax-efficient manner is much better than stockpiling cash in a bank account.

- If you feel comfortable maintaining a simple two-fund account containing a stock and bond index fund, you can stop there. Or you can consider hiring a financial planner to help manage a sliver of your portfolio in alternative investments, like REITs.

- Target retirement date funds and LifeStrategy funds are low-cost options to maintain asset allocation for a small management fee.

HELPFUL RESOURCES

We do not have specific recommendations for financial advisors. There are several resources available online that further describe how to choose a financial advisor and give some examples of "vetted" advisors who may have experience working with physicians. These are:

- https://www.seniorfinanceadvisor.com/resources/how-to-find-a-financial-advisor

- https://www.whitecoatinvestor.com/the-perfect-financial-advisor/

- https://www.whitecoatinvestor.com/financial-advisors/

11

Estate Planning

A goal without a plan is just a wish.
—Antoine de Saint-Exupéry

As your portfolio grows, particularly if you have a family, you may wish to consider hiring an estate planning attorney. Your estate attorney will help you with several important aspects of your estate, including a will, health care proxy, durable power of attorney, and homesteading your house. Some of these things might be self-evident to you, though it might take some time to think through certain specifics, like who will care for your children if you and your spouse are both deceased. Another aspect of estate planning is the formation of various trusts as outlined in this chapter.

You do not need an estate lawyer until you—well— have an estate. And if you plan to live and die with a small estate, you might not need an estate lawyer at all.

Shah CP, Sridhar J. *Financial Freedom Rx:*
The Physician's Guide to Achieving Financial Independence (pp 137-148).
© 2021 SLACK Incorporated.

However, if you espouse the philosophy of growing wealth as a means to achieve financial stability and avoid financial stress, then you may well need an estate lawyer. For such physicians, this might be 5 to 15 years into one's post-training career. A great resource to find an experienced estate lawyer is the website of the American College of Trust and Estate Counsel (https://www.actec.org). ACTEC is a national organization of lawyers who have demonstrated the highest level of professionalism in wills and trust, estate planning, and tax law. As with finding a contractor or a babysitter, word-of-mouth from friends and colleagues can also be an effective way to find a qualified estate lawyer.

At the very least, it is helpful to think about estate planning at the start of your career so you can consider titling your assets separately between you and your spouse if you expect to have a large estate. Separately titled assets are important if you plan to have an estate that might exceed the estate tax limits, and thus you may eventually create revocable trusts for you and your spouse (more on revocable trusts later in the chapter).

Your Will

Your will represents the final wishes you have for your estate. Having a will is a smart idea, particularly if you have children. It allows your desired wishes to be carried out in the event of your death. You can designate who cares for your underaged children in case of your and your spouse's untimely death. And your will gives instructions on how your estate should be distributed. Your wishes may evolve over the course of your life, so you might need to revise your will from time to time. You do not necessarily need an estate lawyer if you only need a basic will and have a simple estate. Online services like Legalzoom.com and Nolo.com can help you write a will.

Upon death, one's estate will often go through a legal process known as probate. Probate determines if the will is authentic and valid, and administers the wishes detailed in it. The probate court will appoint the executor you named in the will, or an administrator if there is no will, to pay off any outstanding liabilities and distribute the assets of the estate. Probate can be a long and expensive process. Furthermore, it is a public process; the value of one's estate is no longer private. It can be very beneficial for the deceased and their heirs to avoid the probate process. An estate lawyer in your state can help you determine if and how your heirs can avoid probate.

HEALTH CARE PROXY

As you know, you might need someone to make rational health care decisions for you, with your wishes and beliefs in mind, should you one day become incapacitated. Your estate lawyer can prepare this document, designating your preferred health care proxy.

DURABLE POWER OF ATTORNEY

Similarly to a health care proxy, you might need a proxy to make legal decisions on your behalf should you become incapacitated. This might be the same person as your health care proxy, or it could be someone else.

HOMESTEADING YOUR HOUSE

Depending on the state in which you live, an estate lawyer can also homestead your house, which protects all or a portion of its value from creditors. In Massachusetts, for example, homesteading your house protects $500,000 of its value, so if someone sues you this amount is protected.

In some states, married couples can own a property by "tenants by entirety." From a liability perspective, this means that creditors who have a claim against one spouse (eg, malpractice case) cannot pursue a jointly held property. However, if the creditor has a claim against both spouses (eg, of slipping on their icy driveway), the jointly held property can be pursued.[1]

ESTATE TAXES

When we die some estates may be subject to estate taxes. Up to a certain amount, one's estate can pass to one's heir free of estate tax. This amount often changes over time depending on how the tax law changes, so it is uncertain what the limit will be when you die. In 2021, the federal limit was $11,700,000 per person and is indexed annually for inflation. This limit was established by the 2017 Tax Cut and Jobs Act and is set to revert to the pre-2018 limits in 2025 but could be extended or otherwise changed by Congress. The estate tax exemption is "portable," which means that if one spouse dies and does not make full use of their exemption, then the surviving spouse can make an election to pick up the unused exemption and add it to the surviving spouse's own exemption. This does require that the executor of the first deceased spouse to pass must file an estate tax return to elect for the portability, which is not automatic. They must file tax form 706 within 9 months of their spouse's death in order to elect portability. This effectively makes the federal exemption \$23,400,000 per married couple.[2] The federal estate tax is 40% for inheritances greater than the limit. There is also estate tax in certain individual states. In Massachusetts, for example, it starts at estates greater than \$1,000,000, with tax rates ranging from 0% to 16%.

Estate laws often change over time, so it is unknown what laws will be in effect at the time of your death. The change in the law in 2010 allowing for portability of the estate tax exemption might be sufficient for some affluent couples. However, there are disadvantages to the portable tax exemption law. For instance, the "ported" amount is static, meaning that it does not continue to grow. So, for instance, if a \$11,700,000 federal estate tax exemption was ported from a deceased spouse, \$23,400,000 of the surviving spouse's estate would be exempt of federal estate tax if they were to die before inflation adjustments to the exemption limits. However, if the exemption amount rose to \$13,000,000 at the time of the surviving spouse's death, their total exemption would be \$11,700,000 plus \$13,000,000, or \$24,700,000. If the couple utilized revocable trusts (see next section), their total estate would have captured the entire \$26,000,000 federal estate tax exemption at the time of their death (\$13,000,000 times two).

Another disadvantage of the portable tax exemption law is that, as of 2019, the state estate tax exemption is not portable in any state except Hawaii and Maryland. Also, if the survivor remarries, the ported amount is lost. Perhaps most importantly, if you do not have a revocable trust and your will goes through probate, it becomes part of the public record, and details of your estate are no longer private.

REVOCABLE TRUSTS

A strategy employed by many wealthy couples in an effort to maximize estate tax limits and maintain privacy utilizes "revocable" or "living" trusts. A revocable trust, or a trust that can be altered or canceled by the grantor, is a "way station" for one's estate to bypass their surviving spouse's estate. In other words, one's individually titled assets would be held in a revocable trust upon one's death and not become part of the surviving spouse's estate. This is why, if you are married and wealthy, it might be prudent to title your and your spouse's accounts separately. If you hold a joint account with a brokerage firm, the joint account can be divided into separately titled accounts between you and your spouse without tax implications.

The money in a revocable trust continues to grow and can be accessed by the surviving spouse or children. For example, if a couple has $22,000,000 between them—$11,000,000 titled in each one's name—when one dies their money passes through to a revocable trust. This can be accessed by their surviving spouse or children. In 2021, there would be no federal estate tax on this amount as it passes to heirs because it is less than the $11,700,000 federal estate tax limit. Further, the surviving spouse's estate remains at $11,000,000, not $22,000,000, thereby not triggering federal estate taxes upon their death. When the surviving spouse eventually dies, the value of their estate grows to $12,000,000 in the revocable trust and $12,000,000 in their estate, and the inflation-adjusted exemption limit at the time of their death rises to $13,000,000, their heirs will not owe federal estate tax because both the revocable trust and the surviving spouse's estate are less than the exemption limit.

If the aforementioned couple in the example lived in Massachusetts, estate taxes would apply to estates greater than $1,000,000. The state tax exemption is not portable to the surviving spouse, which is another reason to consider revocable trusts. If the value of the estate is more than $1,000,000, only the first $40,000 is exempt from state taxes. A progressive tax rate ranging from 0.8% to 16% applies for estate values over $40,000. The maximum 16% state estate tax rate applies to estates worth more than $10,040,000. With revocable trusts, *each* of the spouses' estates, worth over $1,000,000, would not have to pay state estate taxes on $40,000 ($80,000 total), compared to just $40,000 total if the surviving spouse inherited their spouse's half of their wealth without revocable trusts. Further, because of the progressive nature of state estate tax, only the value above $10,040,000 would be subject to the maximum 16% state estate tax. This would be about $1,000,000 ($11,000,000 minus $10,040,000 is about $1,000,000) for each of the spouses' two estates, valued at $11,000,000 each, rather than a 16% tax on $12,000,000 if the combined estate of the surviving spouse was $22,000,000 ($22,000,000 minus $10,040,000 is about $12,000,000). Revocable trusts help most affluent couples minimize federal and state estate taxes so they can leave more of their wealth to their heirs.

There are several advantages to establishing a revocable trust. One of the most important reasons to consider a revocable trust is to maintain privacy. When you die, if all you have is a will, it becomes part of the public record. With a revocable trust, your estate is distributed privately, protecting your heirs and yourself from the potential publicity associated with a large estate. Further, it avoids probate, allowing for faster distribution of your estate to your heirs, and can save money on court fees, which are deducted from your estate.

Not everyone needs a revocable trust. The 2010 portability rule covers most couples whose estates do not exceed federal or state estate tax limits, as long as you do not mind probate and lack of privacy upon your death. Further, if you plan to have little money at your death, or if you plan to give it all to charity, you probably do not need revocable trusts for you and your spouse.

Of course, estate tax laws change regularly. George W. Bush passed the Economic Growth and Tax Relief Reconciliation Act of 2001 (EGTRRA) and the Jobs and Growth Tax Relief Reconciliation Act of 2003 (JGTRRA), which phased out estate taxes entirely in 2010. That would have been a very lucrative year for the wealthy to pass away and leave their entire estate to their heirs. For instance, George Steinbrenner, the owner of the Yankees, died on July 13, 2010, with a net worth of about $1.15 billion. His heirs saved hundreds of millions of dollars in estate taxes. During the following year, 2011, the exclusion amount was $5,000,000 with a maximum tax rate of 35%. In 2020, the exclusion amount was $11,580,000 with a maximum tax rate of 40%. The exclusion amount and the tax rate vary over time, often related to policies of the sitting president. Thus, affluent families should consider appropriate estate planning to minimize estate taxes according to the laws at the time of their deaths.

Individuals should consult an estate lawyer to determine if they should establish revocable trusts in an effort to minimize the tax burden of their estate upon death, maintain privacy for the deceased and for heirs, and avoid probate. If an estate lawyer suggests that you establish revocable trusts, it is not overly expensive to do so. Just be sure to title the estates of each spouse separately, with two separate brokerage accounts. Retirement accounts will already be individually titled. Also, be sure to name beneficiaries appropriately for your accounts. Your trust should be named as the beneficiary for your non-retirement account (taxable brokerage account) and for your Roth accounts (the distributions are not subject to tax). For retirement accounts in which the distributions will be taxed, such as a 401k or individual retirement account (IRA), it is more tax-efficient to name your spouse as the primary beneficiary, because they can roll them over and defer the income tax further.

Of note, a house might be jointly titled. If possible, consider titling it as "tenants by the entirety," in which case the house is protected when a creditor holds a judgment against one spouse (eg, a lawsuit), but not when the judgment is held against both spouses.

IRREVOCABLE TRUSTS

Your estate lawyer can also establish an irrevocable (meaning it can never be revoked or changed) trust. The grantor of the irrevocable trust loses control over any asset or gift placed in it. A designated trustee oversees the irrevocable trust. The grantor dictates the rules of the irrevocable trust, the assets of which can be used by the beneficiary or beneficiaries. There are several advantages to irrevocable trusts:

- This is a vehicle to decrease the size of your estate. For instance, you can put immature investments into an irrevocable trust so that they can grow outside of your estate. These assets are accessible to your beneficiaries in the future if granted approval by your named trustee.

- The grantor can specify certain stipulations before beneficiaries can access the assets within an irrevocable trust.

- An irrevocable trust is shielded from creditors, which may be attractive to physicians in litigious fields.

- The assets of an irrevocable trust are not subject to estate taxes, but gifts of assets into an irrevocable trust that exceed the annual gift tax exclusion limits will count against the lifetime estate and gift tax exclusion (as of 2019, $11,400,000 per individual and indexed for inflation) and require you to file a gift tax return.

- Some people will put a life insurance policy in such a trust to remove death proceeds from the estate. This is called an irrevocable life insurance trust.

- A grantor trust can also be used to deplete one's estate in an effort to be eligible for certain governmental programs like Medicaid for nursing home care.

An irrevocable trust might not be immediately relevant to younger doctors, but it will be worth considering by some later in their careers. It would be worth asking an estate lawyer their opinion based on your specific situation when they are establishing your will, health care proxy, and durable power of attorney.

PEARLS

- Estate planning is something you should consider when you have a growing portfolio and/or a family.

- A will allows your estate to be handled upon your death according to your wishes.

- A health care proxy designates someone to make health care decisions on your behalf in case of your incapacitation.

- A durable power of attorney designates someone to make legal decisions on your behalf in case of your incapacitation.

- Depending on your state of residence, consider either homesteading your house or owning your house with your spouse by "tenants by entirety" to minimize exposure in case of a lawsuit.

- If you think you will have a large portfolio at the time of your death, one that may exceed the estate tax limits at that time, consider either:

  ○ Utilizing the "portability" of the estate tax exemption, so the surviving spouse can effectively double his or her exemption and save on estate taxes for heirs

  ○ Maintaining two identical (or nearly identical) taxable portfolios throughout your life, separately titled each for you and your spouse

- If you think you will exceed the estate tax limits at the time of your death, have your estate lawyer create separate, revocable (also known as "living" or reversible) trusts for each you and your spouse to maximize what can go to your heirs' estate tax-free. This strategy maintains privacy and avoids probate.

- Be sure to name beneficiaries appropriately. Your revocable trust should be the primary beneficiary of your non-retirement accounts (eg, taxable brokerage account) and Roth accounts. Your spouse should be the primary beneficiary of your non-Roth retirement accounts (eg, 401k, IRA) so that they can roll them over and defer income taxes further.

- Consider creating an irrevocable (or irreversible) trust to shield gifts and immature investments to your heirs. The assets of this trust would be controlled by a designated trustee.

We did all the right things. We lived on 20% of our gross income and saved the rest. First, we maximized tax-advantaged accounts, namely our 401ks and 529s for each kid. We even did the backdoor Roth conversion every year. Then, with our excess savings, we opened a joint brokerage account at Fidelity and invested in index funds. After 10 years of practice, we realized that we had grown wealthy. We hired an estate lawyer to help us be smart with our estate. She recommended we split our joint account 50:50, titling each half separately in my name and my husband's. This will allow us to maximize the amount passing to our heirs at the time of our death, based on the expected estate tax limits, while hopefully avoiding the public and prolonged process of probate. Of course, no one can predict when they will die, but we feel comforted knowing that we have prepared our estate in a smart way to minimize estate taxes for our heirs.

REFERENCES

1. LeVine MF. When are spouses' jointly held assets exempt from execution by creditors? Blalock Walters Attorneys at Law. April 8, 2014. Accessed March 16, 2021. https://blalockwalters.com/when-are-spouses-jointly-held-assets-exempt-from-execution-by-creditors/

2. Carlson B. 7 big estate planning mistakes: losing the portability of a spouse's unused exemption. *Forbes.* March 9, 2018. Accessed March 16, 2021. https://www.forbes.com/sites/bobcarlson/2018/03/09/7-big-estate-planning-mistakes-losing-the-portability-of-a-spouses-unused-exemption/?sh=eb17d8e488d3

12

Have I Won the Game?

*A champion needs a motivation above
and beyond winning.*
—Pat Riley

Financial independence is a peaceful place, devoid of the financial stresses that impacted you throughout your training and career. It is important that you understand your annual expenses and how they will evolve over time. Some expenses, such as a house mortgage, college education for your kids, and life insurance, will eventually go away. Other expenses, such as travel, health care, and assisted living, may increase over time. Some expenses are episodic (eg, a car purchase every 4 to 6 years) and may not show up on your yearly analysis of expenses but should be amortized to get a true understanding of your cash flow needs.

Calculating how much money you need to be financially independent must take into account the simultaneous

Shah CP, Sridhar J. *Financial Freedom Rx:*
The Physician's Guide to Achieving Financial Independence (pp 149-156).
© 2021 SLACK Incorporated.

rise in the cost of living and longevity. Historically, amassing 25 times your annual expenses should allow you to withdraw 4% of your portfolio for 30 years. This number might not work if you plan to retire early and live for longer than 30 years in retirement, or if you think your annual expenses might increase in retirement (eg, because you have more time for shopping, travel). Do plan accordingly and amass more (or live on less) if you plan to retire early. And do not forget the impact of taxes. If your annual post-tax expenses amount to $100,000, and you have 25 times this amount, or $2,500,000, saved between a 401k and a taxable index fund account, your post-tax portfolio is significantly lower than $2,500,000 depending on your tax bracket. A more conservative amount would be to amass 33.3 times your annual expenses in taxable accounts rather than 25 times. With 33.3 times your annual expenses, you can pay an effective tax rate of 25% (assuming this is your tax rate in retirement) and still have a net of 25 times your annual expenses. Always allow for some extra wiggle room to handle unexpected expenses once you stop actively earning an income.

To be more granular, online retirement calculators[1] account for the important factors that impact the amount you need to save before achieving financial freedom. Such calculators typically back-calculate from a target monthly income; it is critical to not underestimate the amount one will need in retirement and rather err on the side of overestimating your future expenses. Some investors will stockpile a large cash emergency fund to provide a constant, reliable stream of income in a down market. Utilizing a cash reserve obviates the need to withdraw from an investment account at a loss in a down market, giving the account time to recover.

Financial independence does not necessarily translate into early retirement. But it does translate into early retirement from financial stress and from the conflict of interest inherent in a fee-for-service health care system. Consider using your financial freedom to customize your career while maintaining an income. For example, you may choose to cut back to part-time work or join a teaching institution with a slower pace and lower reimbursement. None of us sacrificed our 20s and our health to become doctors simply for the financial rewards. Without the financial stress of having to see more patients than you wish, see fewer. Connect with them. Hire a scribe to punch data into the electronic medical record so you can do what you love: care for patients. It doesn't matter if your overhead increases and your revenue drops.

> At 64 years old, I am financially independent and as unretired as one could be. I worked at an academic center my whole career, seeing lots of patients, hustling in clinic, and operating late. Now, I still work full-time at the same hospital, but in a much more enjoyable capacity, supervising resident clinics and surgeries. My salary is much less than before, but the extra income is a bonus given I am already set up for "retirement." The patients are underprivileged and uninsured for the most part, adding a component of charity to my work, and working with residents keeps me young and fresh. The biggest honor of my career was receiving the resident teaching award last year from the graduating residency class; devoting this much time

and energy to my passion for education would be impossible without my financial independence, given that education realistically does not pay as well as clinical productivity. Plus, I take time off to travel with my wife every couple of months without worrying about the "lost income" while on vacation. Frankly, my work–life balance has never been better!

Winning the game is not ultimately about saving money. Building wealth confers flexibility to create the life you want for yourself, your spouse, and your children. Experiences that may once have been prohibitively expensive now become possible, because once you have achieved financial independence, everything you make in excess is expendable. You can spend that excess on anything you want, including experiences like great vacations or material things like fancy clothes. Just do not recalibrate your quality of life so your expenses remain inflated when you stop working! You can donate generously to charity to leave a lasting legacy and impact organizations you hold dear. You may elect to leave some assets for your heirs for future opportunities such as higher education expenses, a house, or start-up funding for a business. Regardless of how you choose to spend your excess income, financial independence confers on you the freedom to make choices in line with the purpose and goals of your personal life.

We were so frugal as a young couple with kids, rarely going on vacation beyond a drive to a local beach town. We never ate out at restaurants, and my husband and I squirreled away every penny.

Now we are both retired from clinical medicine and have more wealth than we can spend before we go. We have invested in our children and grandchildren; we are covering college tuition for the grandkids, and we take the whole crew of 18 on an annual family trip that has created invaluable memories, bonding, and experiences. I have some regrets about not taking our own children on trips when they were younger, but we had a different mindset then, and it's a lot easier to spend money when you know you have enough!

PEARLS

- Financial independence affords financial peace, knowing that you can live the rest of your days without relying on an active income.

- Without dependence on a paycheck, you can adjust your lifestyle accordingly. Some may work less, spend more time teaching, or participate in humanitarian work.

- When you amass 33.3 times your annual expenses in pre-tax dollars, or 25 times in post-tax dollars, you can draw 4% per year for 30 years.

- If you plan to retire early, and stop earning a paycheck, you will need to either amass a larger portfolio or live more modestly to make it more than 30 years without running out of money. Use online retirement calculators to play with the variables of time and expenses.

- Once you have enough to live without a paycheck for 30 or more years, everything you make in excess can be spent, donated, or left as an inheritance.

To me as a "retiring" MD at 57 years old, this is the most important section of any financial planning book. What truly does "enough" mean? I always think back to when I was younger. I used to study chess, and chess books would describe the differences between playing with tactics and playing with strategy. Playing with tactics implies playing move-to-move the best move you see on the board, utilizing the pieces you currently have at your disposal. Playing with strategy implies long-term planning, where you see the end goal you would like to achieve and then work backward to figure out the steps necessary to get there. You can win at chess playing either way, and the same is true in life, but I would argue that true personal fulfillment really comes from strategic rather than tactical maneuvering. I feel that as physicians we are very well developed at the day-to-day tasks of working hard, coming in early and staying up late to help patients, booking cases, and just grinding—in other words, at tactical thinking. We are less good at understanding where we are going and how what we do on a daily basis factors into a strategic vision.

When it comes to finances, all of the tactics discussed in this book are invaluable, like automatic investing or tax-loss harvesting, but happiness does not come from having a lot of money in a retirement account. It took me until now to figure out what I truly want to do with my life now that I am financially independent: I kept enough in the bank to maintain my financial independence, closed my practice, and launched a health care technology start-up. I work not to make more money but because I am passionate about the product and ideas my start-up is promoting. So, for me, "enough" means having the opportunity to pursue one's true passion, whatever that may be. You cannot plan for everything to come, so do your best and don't sweat the small stuff. Figure out how to save enough and then spend your remaining money, time, and energy on spending time and creating memories with your loved ones. Figure out when you will have enough and why it is important to you in terms of further creating the life you want to live, not the life you feel you have to live. Figuring that out early is probably the wisest thing any young doctor could do. Then you can use the tactics you possess to achieve your long-term vision.

Reference

1. Retirement calculator. Bankrate. Accessed March 16, 2021. https://www.bankrate.com/calculators/retirement/retirement-plan-calculator/

13

Retirement Distributions

Retirement is wonderful if you have two essentials:
much to live on and much to live for.
—Unknown

Retirement is a relative term. For some it is defined in the traditional sense, marked by the abrupt cessation of work in one's twilight years. For others, retirement represents a more gradual transition, with a slow relinquishment of responsibilities and time spent at work. Whatever it means for you, retirement is typically the time to start withdrawing from the portfolio you built during your working years. Depending on your individual situation, tapping your various savings accounts in the most tax-efficient manner can be somewhat complex. This is a good time to consult a tax advisor and study resources dedicated to the topic, like *The Bogleheads' Guide to Retirement Planning*. Herein, we will briefly review the

Shah CP, Sridhar J. *Financial Freedom Rx:*
The Physician's Guide to Achieving Financial Independence (pp 157-164).
© 2021 SLACK Incorporated.

principles one must consider in retirement to develop an efficient strategy of accessing savings accounts and maintaining adequate cash flow.

BUDGET

A budget continues to be important throughout life, particularly in retirement or semiretirement. As with all budgets, expenses evolve over time. Some expenses, like health care or travel, can rise, while others, like housing, can fall, if one is downsizing or if the mortgage is already paid off. You'll want to keep track of your annual household budget so that you can determine how much you will need to withdraw from your portfolio each year.

BASELINE INCOME

Although almost everyone experiences a commensurate reduction in earned income when they are partially or completely retired, most retirees continue to maintain a certain income stream from other sources. These sources can include dividends, interest, rental income, Social Security, pensions, annuities, and earnings from other investments or business endeavors.

Add up all of your income from such sources and subtract this total from your annual expenses. The difference is the amount of your portfolio you must liquidate each year to live your life. As discussed in Chapter 12, this amount should be less than 4% of the value of your portfolio. If you are drawing more than 4% of your portfolio, you must consider living a more modest lifestyle, earning more money, or both if you want your portfolio to last 30 years. On the other hand, if your baseline income in retirement covers your annual budget, obviating the need to touch your portfolio, you are free to live it up and spend some money!

REQUIRED MINIMUM DISTRIBUTIONS

The government will not let you keep your tax-advantaged accounts forever, and thus there are required minimum distributions (RMDs) from simplified employee pension individual retirement account (SEP-IRA), traditional IRA, rollover IRA, and workplace savings accounts (401k, 403b, 457). Roth plans are not subject to RMDs.

The first RMD must be withdrawn by April 1 in the year following one's 70½ birthday (if born before July 1, 1949) or 72nd birthday (if born after June 30, 1949). There are worksheets on the Internal Revenue Service website to help you determine what percentage you must withdraw, based on life expectancy and account value.[1]

The second and all subsequent RMDs are due on December 31. If you take your first RMD between January 1 and April 1, and your second before the end of the year, you will have two RMDs within the same calendar year. This increases your tax burden and can put you in a higher tax bracket. Keep in mind that RMDs are taxed as ordinary income, not as more favorable capital gains. Consider taking the first RMD in the same calendar year you turn 70½ or 72 to avoid having to take two RMDs in the same year.

RMDs can significantly increase a retiree's taxable income at a time when they might not need the money or want the associated tax burden. One strategy to minimize RMDs is to convert money from traditional retirement accounts to Roth accounts, which are not subject to RMDs. As you know, Roth accounts are funded with post-tax dollars, grow tax-free, and can be withdrawn without tax consequence. However, one must pay taxes when converting a traditional retirement account to a Roth account. Oftentimes, retirees will have low income early in retirement, placing them in a lower tax bracket and possibly creating an ideal opportunity for a Roth conversion. Keep in mind that new retirees often defer the start of Social Security payments early in retirement, thus keeping their income low as they live off savings. As an extra bonus, deferring Social Security payments boosts the eventual monthly benefit.

If you are in a lower tax bracket between the ages of 59½ and 70½ or 72, it might make sense to withdraw some money from your IRA, even if you do not need it. This allows you to lower your eventual RMD, and also to pay less tax than you would later when you might be in a higher tax bracket. If you do not think you will need some or all of your RMD, this low tax bracket period might be a good opportunity for a Roth conversion.

Another way to reduce one's tax burden is to make an IRA charitable contribution whereby you directly transfer up to $100,000 from your IRA to your favorite charity. You do not pay taxes on this donation and it satisfies the RMD for the year. You can contribute a partial amount or your entire RMD.

PENALTIES

There are significant consequences of not taking an RMD, namely a penalty of 50% of the value of your RMD. Ouch. Keep in mind that retirement account RMDs from a 401k or 403b can be deferred until you retire if you are still working after the age of 70½ or 72 and do not own 5% or more of the company for which you work. This is not true for IRA RMDs, which must be taken after your 70½ or 72nd birthday, regardless of your employment status.

There are also penalties for early withdrawal. Withdrawal from a traditional IRA or 401k/403b before the age of 59½ results in a 10% penalty. One can take 401k withdrawal without penalty at age 55 if one leaves the job associated with that workplace savings account at or after age 55. There is no penalty for early withdrawal from a 457 plan.

SINGLE PREMIUM IMMEDIATE ANNUITY

For many, income generated from Social Security, dividends, interest, and RMDs will be sufficient to cover one's expenses in retirement. For some, particularly for those who feel they might outlive their money, a fixed single premium immediate annuity (SPIA) is an insurance product that pays you a set amount for the rest of your life, much like a pension. Consider discussing this type of annuity with your financial advisor early in retirement to help you determine if it is right for you.

WITHDRAWAL STRATEGIES

There is no one right way of withdrawing money for retirement from your portfolio's various accounts. When you are considering the best tax strategy for you in retirement, and for your heirs upon your death, speak with your tax advisor. There are two general approaches, based on whether you want to (1) minimize your taxes, or (2) minimize your heirs' taxes.

Minimizing Your Taxes

A tax sensitive strategy for withdrawing money starts with taxable accounts. The dividends and interest from this account are already taxed, so spend that money first. If and when you need to start selling the principal, consider selling enough in an upmarket to support 1 to 3 years of expenses. Place this amount in a low-risk bucket, such as a money market fund. This way you are not forced to liquidate part of your portfolio in a down market. Further, the remaining principal can continue to grow at market rates for future use.

The next source for income is your Roth account, whether that be your Roth IRA or Roth 401k. This amount is tax-free and has no minimum distribution requirement.

The third income source is your tax-deferred account, such as an IRA or traditional 401k. Remember, you will already be taking annual RMD distributions when you reach 70½ or 72 years of age, and these distributions are taxed as ordinary income. If you need more income than afforded by your taxable or Roth accounts, take a distribution from your tax-deferred account(s), leaving what you do not need in the account to grow.

Minimizing Your Heirs' Taxes

Some fortunate people, and hopefully many reading this book, will amass a small fortune by retirement. They might be able to support their retirement lifestyle with savings, passive income (eg, Social Security, dividends, rental income), and RMDs. For these people who will likely bequeath a sizeable portfolio, there are some general strategies to minimize taxes for heirs. A taxable account is a good account to pass on, as the cost basis "resets." For example, if you purchase Vanguard Total Stock Market Index Fund Admiral Shares (VTSAX) for $60, and the value rises to $100 upon your passing, then the cost basis for your heirs resets to $100. This means they do not have to pay taxes on the $40 gain, but they will have to pay taxes when they sell on any gains beyond the newly reset $100 basis.

Roth accounts are also good accounts to pass to heirs, as they will not pay taxes on withdrawals. One caveat is that the Roth account must be open for at least 5 years before the account holder dies, otherwise their heirs will owe taxes on the earnings at the time of withdrawal.

PEARLS

- Maintaining tax-efficient cash flow in retirement requires planning and a good understanding of your evolving budget.
- Your annual expenses minus your baseline income from Social Security, dividends, interest, and other income streams equal the amount you will have to liquidate from your portfolio each year.
- Understand your RMDs from your non-Roth IRA and workplace retirement accounts.
- Consider converting some of your IRA or 401k to a Roth plan in early retirement when you might be in a lower tax bracket, in an effort to reduce your RMDs when you turn 70½ or 72.
- Take your RMDs, even if you do not need them, so you do not have to pay stiff penalties.
- Consider investing a lump sum into a fixed SPIA if you are worried that you might outlive your money.

- Consider withdrawing from your retirement accounts in the following sequence to be the most tax-efficient for yourself: taxable accounts, Roth accounts, tax-deferred accounts.

- Consider bequeathing your taxable accounts so the cost basis resets, and your Roth accounts so your heirs do not have to pay taxes on withdrawals, if you wish to minimize taxes for your heirs upon your death.

- Consult your tax advisor to determine the best withdrawal strategy for your individual situation to minimize taxes for you and your heirs.

REFERENCE

1. Required minimum distribution worksheets. Internal Revenue Service. Accessed March 16, 2021. https://www.irs.gov/retirement-plans/plan-participant-employee/required-minimum-distribution-worksheets

14

Pitfalls to Avoid

*A smart man makes a mistake, learns from it,
and never makes that mistake again.
But a wise man finds a smart man and learns from
him how to avoid the mistake altogether.*
—**Roy H. Williams**

You will make mistakes along your path to financial independence. All of us do. But keep the mistakes small and few, and keep working hard to learn and adjust from any missteps. Here are a few to try and avoid:

1. Do Not Let Delayed Gratification Lure You Into a Trap That Leads to Delayed Retirement

Live below your means. Remember that "enough" is absolute, not relative. Find happiness with enough.

Shah CP, Sridhar J. *Financial Freedom Rx:*
The Physician's Guide to Achieving Financial Independence (pp 165-176).
© 2021 SLACK Incorporated.

As a surgeon, I felt embarrassed walking to the parking lot with the anesthesiologist, headed toward my beat-up Subaru from residency while he hopped into his BMW. I felt that to be successful I had to maintain an image of success. And I had been making sacrifices my whole life to get where I was. "Treat yourself," right? So, I bought a very nice but very expensive Range Rover. It was the ultimate status symbol. I loved it at first, though I quickly realized it was not practical for a city, nor affordable. It was really hard to find an adequate parking spot, and I was always worried it would get dinged. The upkeep expenses and monthly payments were killer. It cost $80 to fill the tank! And every few months there was some maintenance expense. I realized that I was happier and wealthier with my beater car, never having to worry about a new ding or expensive maintenance. I didn't need a fancy car to be a great surgeon.

2. Consider Owning Only One Home

It can be tempting to own a second home, perhaps a summer house on the lake or a mountain lodge on the slopes. For some, it may actually make financial sense to do so, if one needs to spend a lot of time in a second location or if the second property is a profitable rental when not being used. But for most, a second mortgage and the upkeep costs of a second home can be a drain on one's finances, not to mention one's time. Never let your possessions own you.

> My husband is a dermatologist, and I am an ophthalmologist. In our 40s we bought a condominium on the water in addition to our actual home. We figured it would be a good investment to rent and that one day our kids could have it. It turned out to be a monster financial drain between upkeep costs, hurricane damage and insurance, and problems with tenants. Then our kids decided to leave town to work elsewhere! We ended up selling the condo 10 years after purchase to cut our losses. We still are doing well financially, but that money could have better spent in so many other ways, even on multiple nice vacations, over the past decade.

3. TRY NOT TO GET DIVORCED

Unfortunately, about half of Americans get divorced, with divorce rates varying between medical fields.[1] Divorce is quietly one of the biggest financial (and emotional) calamities one will face in life. It is a 50% bear market that you may never recover from financially. Wellness and work–life balance throughout your training and career will hopefully allow for a healthy, lifelong marriage. Have a low threshold to invest in marriage counseling before things get bad. Money is a common source of friction in a marriage. Mismatched expectations or spending habits can introduce conflict into a marriage. Communicate about these matters early and often.

One of my orthopedic surgery fellowship attendings was still grinding away in his 60s. He would do more surgeries and add-on weekend cases more than any other attending. He also would be a big spender and take us and others out for nice dinners and drinks all the time. We assumed that he must just enjoy the work and be very well off, but some days he seemed "over it" yet still kept going. My co-fellows and I finally found out why from a nurse in the operating room: turns out he was paying for three divorces, so even though he would have preferred to be retired, it was not anywhere on the horizon. He was also essentially living paycheck to paycheck given his expensive habits. That gave us all pause and was really sobering. Divorce seems like the most expensive mistake a physician can make.

4. Consider Keeping One Job

Once you have done it, you appreciate the opportunity costs associated with finding a job. Though half of physicians will leave their first job due to geographic needs, better opportunities, job dissatisfaction, or for other reasons, it is more efficient financially to invest as much time and thought in choosing the right job first of all. But, if your dream job finally becomes available, do your homework and make the transition if it is the right decision.

I will be the first to admit that I chose my first job poorly. It offered a high starting salary that was enticing, and I figured I could live in a small town and make bank within 10 years. The only problem was I did not do my due diligence into the practice owners and later felt they did not treat me fairly or ethically. Also, I was living in an area that made me unhappy from day one. I left that job within 2 years and ended up as an associate in a practice near my hometown. I am now a partner and very happy with how things worked out. My only regret is that I could have been partner 2 years earlier and applied that "sweat equity" toward my current job.

5. Do Not Carry High-Interest Debt

Most medical students will graduate with debt; it's part of the game. The key is to not let the debt linger as a financial albatross hanging around your neck. Once you have retired your medical school debt, your goal should be to remain as debt-free as possible going forward. All too often, physicians become all too comfortable carrying debt, damaging both their credit and their opportunity to accumulate wealth.

My parents used only debit cards when I was growing up; as immigrants they were suspicious of credit card companies and terrified of debt. As a result, I was never well educated about credit cards, and they were almost my undoing. Even though I paid off my medical school debt, I was carrying high amounts of credit card debt well into my 40s without fully understanding the terms. I had opened some cards that did not charge interest in the first year, and then somehow thought they were interest-free long-term as long as I made the minimum payment. I had other cards with high annual fees that had great perks for opening an account; the only problem was that 7 years later I was still paying those annual fees. Things came to a head when I got married, and my new wife discovered my mess of credit card debt and my ugly credit score. My new wife almost became my new ex-wife, but we worked things out and she showed me how much trouble I was actually in. Don't get comfortable with debt; you don't need it at all to be financially stable and happy!

6. Do Not Lose Patience or Get Bored

Winning the game is not about style points or flair. Minimizing fees and taxes while earning the market return by investing steadily in low-cost index funds is a sure-fire way to outperform most investors, yet doctors often struggle to stick to the plan. Lack of patience and boredom play a huge role. The market may fluctuate, but do not wander off the path. Remember, being the tortoise is not always sexy, but crossing the financial finish line earlier is exciting and liberating. Be a sexy tortoise.

When I started investing I treated it like I treat my fantasy football team. Always look for the hot "player," dump the poorly performing ones, and live and die week to week. Well, it turns out that an exciting investment life is not necessarily the most financially healthy. I lost close to $20,000 my first year of investing, not including the commissions I was paying for individual stock transactions. Now my money is parked in index funds, and I get all of my thrills with an extra $10 buy-in for a second fantasy football team. It has been a little friendlier to my wallet.

7. Avoid High Downside Investments

The deadly cousin of lack of patience is speculation, where a fantastic, huge return opportunity comes your way that you simply cannot pass up—and then you take a financial hit, setting your plan back years. The opportunity for massive returns is tantalizing until you remember that the potential for high reward is coupled with high risk. As a high earner, your job is simple: save and do not lose. Resist FOMO—fear of missing out. If you really want to gamble with your money, take a small fixed amount and go to Vegas for the weekend. And if, in retrospect, you missed a speculative opportunity that posted a big return, just remember the other nine that went bust.

Everyone has a financial weakness, and for me, it was Bitcoin. I was dollar-cost investing and gradually building wealth Boglehead-style, but when my friends started texting on a group thread about the possible returns with cryptocurrencies, I started fantasizing about being financially independent within a couple of years. I never pulled money out of investments, thankfully, but I did pour almost $20,000 into an investment that had already reached its peak. I forgot every rule I apply to individual stocks when I smirk at colleagues discussing the latest hot tip investment. Pride cometh before the fall! Two years later my investment is worth half of what it was initially. It hurts every time I do the math and think how that money would have compounded in a simple index fund.

8. Do Not Overpay Someone to Do Your Financial Planning

Physicians are certainly capable of managing their own finances. Just as you earn continuing medical education credits each year to stay cutting edge, read at least one financial book every year. Becoming financially literate and fluent will help you both professionally (managing your practice) and personally (managing your wealth). And keep your finances simple, utilizing workplace savings accounts, index funds, and automatic investing as described. Financial planners can be helpful educators, but be wary of the conflict of interest inherent in every investment vehicle they sell. The least biased advice may come from an advisor who charges an annual or one-time fee and is not conflicted by commission. In our opinion, think twice before paying someone a percentage of your assets per year, in both up and down markets, to manage your portfolio. The more you pay, the less you keep. And over decades, that fee snowballs into colossal proportions. But for some, a management fee is a fair price to pay compared to having no plan, no oversight, and no execution. Be sure the fees you pay are commensurate to the value you get from a financial advisor. Or consider low-cost target retirement date funds or fixed asset allocation funds that have low expense ratios.

There's a big difference between fee-based and fee-only advisors. I thought I was signing up for a fee-only advisor, one who presumably did not have a conflict of interest and could give me unbiased financial advice. But, it turns out he was fee-based. So, in addition to charging me an annual fee, he made a commission on the products in which I invested. Aside from being expensive, with hidden commission fees, it was hard for me to trust his advice due to his significant conflict of interest. For my overall financial plan, would he encourage me to pay off my educational debt and maximize my 401k contributions when neither of these investments would benefit him?

9. Learn the Business of Medicine

It is critical to understand basic coding and reimbursement and how it applies to your specific subspecialty. Replacing sloppy or suboptimal billing with good, ethical, and legal coding can add up to thousands of dollars each year without changing your work flow or the quality of care you are delivering. Understanding the basics of health care management will repay you in spades as you make your practice efficient and productive.

In-depth discussion of medical coding and billing is beyond the scope of this book, but at the very least one should understand which Current Procedural Terminology (CPT) codes are most utilized in your specialty and when they should be applied. Documentation in your chart, whether it is the emergency room, clinic, or the operating room, has to be sufficient to justify a CPT code both in terms of diagnoses managed and complexity. Just as important is understanding modifiers. Modifiers are added to a CPT code to add information regarding a procedure and service and are critical in certain scenarios to get reimbursed appropriately, especially in the setting of another recent medical procedure. Adding the correct modifier could be the difference between getting paid the full amount for a procedure and absolutely nothing!

I did my residency at an academic university where we were not really taught coding or billing as residents; I always assumed it was above our pay grade, and honestly, it was easier to get through a clinic day without worrying about it. We would all just click "level 3" for every clinic visit and never bothered to place the correct orders for in-office procedures. We dictated operative notes, but half of the time the procedures did not match the billing diagnoses. Then I did a fellowship at a private practice where they oriented us on billing, gave us mandatory homework to read, and expected us to bill and code correctly when working with the attendings. It was painful and one of my least favorite parts of the job, but it ended up being the most valuable part of the fellowship education. When I graduated and went back to the same institution of my residency education as a faculty member, I realized that no one had taught us billing as residents because almost none of the faculty knew how! By billing correctly and efficiently, I worked at a normal rate and still rapidly moved up the ladder financially at my institution, allowing me more senior privileges at an early stage of my career. I also spoke to the leadership at our institution and helped educate faculty and residents about simple ways to improve billing and get correctly reimbursed for the services we provided. The thing to remember about medical coding and billing is that it is never static. I would tell anyone who fails to understand the importance of coding to invest time in attending a course in your specialty and stay current, as the rules are ever-changing!

10. Actually Do Financial Planning

Put this book down, grab your computer, and get at it. It is easy to put this off until the weekend or your next vacation, but there is no better time than the present. Follow the checklist in Appendix A, start living below your means, get your family on board, and change the trajectory of your life.

> Financial planning has always made me uncomfortable and nervous. On my free weekends I would always rather read the radiology journals than sit down and open my own investment account. I put it off for years due to being afraid of doing it "wrong." My sister finally sat me down one weekend when she was visiting, and it took all of 10 minutes to get my initial and automatic investments set up. I realized that as long as you keep it simple, efficient, automated, and low-cost, there is no "wrong." Now I still spend my weekends paging through the journals, but at least my money is working for me in the background. Sometimes the initial activation energy to get started is the toughest part. As doctors we are used to being experts, and it is uncomfortable feeling like a novice, but break past that discomfort and you will find the basics are not so hard to understand.

Reference

1. Ly DP, Seabury SP, Jena AB. Divorce among physicians and other health-care professionals in the United States: analysis of census survey data. *BMJ.* 2015;350:h706. https://www.bmj.com/content/350/bmj.h706

Epilogue

It takes some strategic planning early in your career, and periodically throughout it, to establish a sound financial plan and achieve great wealth. It starts with you adopting the philosophy that you can have a good life while living below your means. And it requires discipline to save and invest regularly.

We hope that the preceding 14 chapters will serve as a helpful guide for you as you chart your financial growth. The checklist in Appendix A is a roughly chronological approach to the tasks you need to complete as your career progresses and your wealth grows. This guide is intended to be a reference you will revisit periodically as well as a starting point for further financial education. There is always more to learn. And finance, like medicine, is an

Shah CP, Sridhar J. *Financial Freedom Rx:*
The Physician's Guide to Achieving Financial Independence (pp 177-178).
© 2021 SLACK Incorporated.

ever-changing landscape that requires periodic "continuing education" to reinforce concepts while learning new tactics. In Appendix B we have listed several helpful financial resources that should be added to your reading list. As physicians, educators, and students ourselves, we thank you for giving us the opportunity to contribute to your education.

Always remember that "enough" is absolute, not relative. Live a good life, with enough to make you happy. Have luxuries, too; you earned them. But remember that great freedom accompanies financial stability. Continue to educate yourself about personal finance with the same discipline that got you to where you are today. We hope that once you are on track to financial independence you can be mentally free to focus on the things most important to you personally. Good luck!

—*Chirag P. Shah, MD, MPH*
—*Jayanth Sridhar, MD*

Appendix A

Checklist

☐ Choose a medical specialty that you love and that will grow with you throughout life. When torn between more than one option, consider your future quality of life in terms of hours, stress, and income level.

☐ Get a great job you love in a location you love. Plan to never leave.

☐ Contemplate (with your significant other, if applicable) your life philosophy. How do you want to live on the spectrum of living large (paycheck to paycheck) or living modestly but accumulating great wealth and peace of mind? Everyone's balance is based on their inherent values and may well evolve over time.

Shah CP, Sridhar J. *Financial Freedom Rx:*
The Physician's Guide to Achieving Financial Independence (pp 179-183).
© 2021 SLACK Incorporated.

☐ Make a budget that you will continue to evolve as you and your life evolve. Budget your savings first and spend what remains. You can use Quicken or another similar software or online program to help you budget. Credit card and bank statements can often help you understand your spending.

☐ Create a financial plan that both you and your spouse can support, including spending guidelines.

☐ Get disability insurance when you are still young and healthy with the following riders: own-occupation, guaranteed insurability, residual disability, and guaranteed renewal. Consider a cost-of-living rider, particularly while you are still young. Increase your coverage as your salary grows.

☐ Evaluate your high-interest student loans. Pay them off first, or refinance to a rate worth maintaining until maturity.

☐ Maximize your workplace retirement savings account (eg, 401k, 403b) to the amount that is matched so you capitalize on free money. After that, maximize your workplace savings beyond the match to the annual IRS limits.

☐ Consider a Roth 401k if it is offered by your employer and if you think you will always be in the top tax bracket, are able to contribute more money to retirement now, and value tax diversification in retirement.

☐ If you do not think you will be in a lower tax bracket in retirement, then consider an after-tax backdoor Roth IRA conversion for you and your spouse every year to save more money for retirement in a tax-advantaged vehicle. Set a reminder in your phone to do a backdoor Roth IRA each year.

☐ Consider opening a 529 educational account for each child and contribute up to the maximum gifting amount ($30,000 per couple per child in 2021) until you reach a total value that works for your child(ren)'s anticipated educational expenses.

☐ If you earn any income as a sole proprietor or independent contractor, recorded on Form 1099, consider opening a self-employed 401k (instead of a SEP-IRA) to further save for retirement in a tax-efficient manner while still allowing annual backdoor Roth IRA conversions. By being able to participate in a backdoor Roth IRA, you will be able to tuck away post-tax dollars that grow tax-free and are not taxed upon withdrawal.

☐ When you are ready to buy a house, consider a 15-year fixed mortgage rather than a 30-year, both to save money in the long run and to eliminate debt sooner.

☐ Consider a 20- or 30-year term life insurance plan to cover future expenses, your mortgage, and your kids' college expenses, in the event of your untimely death.

Once you have completed or considered the aforementioned tasks, then:

☐ Consider opening a taxable brokerage account to save
more money once you have maximized tax-advantaged
accounts. (Your estate lawyer might suggest splitting a
joint account into two separate accounts each for you
and your spouse that are separately titled for estate
planning purposes.)

☐ Link your checking account to your brokerage account.

☐ Set up automatic investments so that you are
contributing to your brokerage accounts on a regular
basis (weekly or monthly) and so you benefit from
dollar cost averaging.

☐ Choose investment funds based on your preferences.
Strongly consider a low-cost total stock market index
fund as your core holding.

☐ As your portfolio grows, diversify into other
investments such as bonds, international stocks,
and REITs.

☐ Periodically rebalance by evaluating your overall asset
allocation twice a year.

☐ Periodically tax-loss harvest.

☐ Use online resources, such as eMoney offered by
Fidelity, or Quicken, to understand your savings,
spending, and investment diversification and growth.

☐ Do not make speculative investments. You are on track
to winning the game if you stay the course. Be the
tortoise, not the hare.

☐ You can consider hiring a financial advisor if you feel they would be helpful and allow you access to alternative investments such as municipal bond ladders and REITs. Keep in mind that many such investments are only available to accredited investors (net worth > $1,000,000, or annual income more than $200,000 [$300,000 if married] for 3 years) or qualified purchasers (investments > $5,000,000). A financial advisor should also help you be as tax efficient as possible and become more conservative as you get older. Consider one who charges a flat fee for advice and guidance rather than one who charges a certain percentage of your portfolio to manage it. Remember, fees are sometimes negotiable, especially as your portfolio grows.

☐ Early on, hire an estate lawyer to draft your will, health care proxy, and power of attorney. Depending on your state and personal situation, they might also recommend homesteading your house to protect some or all of it from creditors. They may also create revocable trusts to avoid probate, provide privacy and potentially reduce estate taxes upon your death, and possibly establish an irrevocable trust for immature investments to grow outside your estate. You should carefully link the ownership of your various financial assets (eg, house, investments, retirement accounts, insurance policies) and the beneficiaries with your legal documents and trusts, keeping in mind the tax implications both now and in the future.

☐ Periodically evaluate if you have won the game and are financially independent. Do you have at least 25 to 33 times your annual expenses? Isn't freedom grand?

Appendix B

Resources

We find that managing the financial productivity and success of a medical practice has similarities to managing your personal financial affairs. Investing in education on how to manage a medical practice has crossover benefits to managing your personal finances and frequently will pay for itself quite quickly. Often, subspecialty organizations will have "Business of Medicine"–type seminars or meetings that can be invaluable to refresh on billing, coding, and practice management.

If you wish to go beyond what we covered in this guidebook, following is a list of recommended resources (books, websites, podcasts) to further supplement your education. We strongly encourage you to keep up with your financial education with ongoing reading and learning.

Shah CP, Sridhar J. *Financial Freedom Rx:*
The Physician's Guide to Achieving Financial Independence (pp 185-189).
© 2021 SLACK Incorporated.

INVESTING

- *The Most Important Thing: Uncommon Sense for the Thoughtful Investor* by Howard Marks
- *The Intelligent Investor* by Benjamin Graham
- *The Elements of Investing: Easy Lessons for Every Investor* by Burton G. Malkiel and Charles D. Ellis
- *The Bogleheads' Guide to Investing* by Mel Lindauer, Taylor Larimore, and Michael LaBoeuf
- *A Random Walk Down Wall Street* by Burton G. Malkiel
- *Unconventional Success: A Fundamental Approach to Personal Investment* by David F. Swensen
- Warren Buffett's letters to Berkshire Hathaway shareholders: https://www.berkshirehathaway.com/letters/letters.html
- *Common Stocks and Uncommon Profits* by Philip A. Fisher
- *Expected Returns: An Investor's Guide to Harvesting Market Rewards* by Antti Ilmanen
- *Adaptive Markets: Financial Evolution at the Speed of Thought* by Andrew W. Lo
- *The Only Investment Guide You'll Ever Need* by Andrew Tobias

DIRECTLY WRITTEN FOR MEDICAL PROVIDERS

- *The White Coat Investor: A Doctor's Guide to Personal Finance and Investing* by James M. Dahle, MD

- *The White Coat Investor's Financial Boot Camp* by James M. Dahle, MD
- *The White Coat Investor's Guide for Students: How Medical and Dental Students Can Secure Their Financial Future* by James M. Dahle, MD
- *The Physician Philosopher's Guide to Personal Finance: The 20% of Personal Finance Doctors Need to Know to Get 80% of the Results* by James D. Turner, MD

Personal Finance

- *The Automatic Millionaire* by David Bach
- *Your Money or Your Life* by Vicki Robin
- *The Millionaire Next Door: The Surprising Secrets of America's Wealthy* by Thomas J. Stanley and William D. Danko

Business/Negotiation

- *The Essays of Warren Buffett: Lessons for Corporate America* by Lawrence A. Cunningham
- *Never Split the Difference: Negotiating as if Your Life Depended on It* by Chris Voss
- *Exactly What to Say: The Magic Words for Influence and Impact* by Phil M. Jones
- *Getting to Yes: Negotiating Agreement Without Giving In* by Roger Fisher and William Ury

MISCELLANEOUS FINANCE

- *The Eternity Portfolio, Illuminated: A Practical Guide to Investing Your Money for Ultimate Results* by Alan Gotthardt
- *Give Smart: Philanthropy That Gets Results* by Thomas J. Tierney and Joel L. Fleishman
- *Raising Financially Fit Kids* by Joline Godfrey

WEBSITES

- Bogleheads: http://bogleheads.org

  A terrific resource filled with investing advice inspired by John Bogle. The forums are a great place to ask questions and get a sense of what "enough" means for different successful savers.

- Physician on FIRE: http://www.physicianonfire.com

  A personal finance website put together by an anesthesiologist who successfully achieved financial independence before age 40 filled with excellent blog posts, financial calculators, and weekly links to other financial resources.

- The White Coat Investor: http://www.whitecoatinvestor.com

  Dr. James Dahle is an emergency medicine physician who used to frequent the bogleheads.org forum and started his own website with a blog, courses, and forum with well-written, clear, and easy-to-understand articles ranging from "beginner" to "expert" level. Follow on social media (Facebook and Twitter, @WCInvestor).

Podcasts

- *Financial Residency* by Ryan Inman
- *The Freedom Formula for Physicians* by Dave Denniston
- *Dr. Money Matters* by Dr. Tarang Patel
- *The White Coat Investor Podcast* by Dr. James Dahle

INDEX